INTERNET SPY

BY
IAN PROBERT

Kingfisher
NEW YORK

KINGFISHER
Larousse Kingfisher Chambers Inc.
95 Madison Avenue
New York, New York 10016

First edition 1996
10 9 8 7 6 5 4 3 2

LIBRARY OF CONGRESS CATALOGING-IN-PUBLICATION DATA

Probert, Ian
    Internet spy/Ian Probert
        —1st American ed.   p.   cm.—(Classified)
    Summary: Relates a 1989 incident of German computer hackers being
paid by the KGB to break into top secret computer files in the
United States.
    1. Computer crimes. Case studies. Juvenile literature.
[1. Computer crimes. 2. Espionage]
I. Title. II. Series.
HV6773.P76 1996 364.1'68'092—dc20
[B] 96–173 CIP AC

ISBN 0-7534-5007-0

Printed and bound in Great Britain by
Cox & Wyman Ltd, Reading, Berkshire

CONTENTS PAGE

INTRODUCTION

Murder; possibly the oldest crime on Earth. Computer hacking; possibly the newest. Put them together and the result is an incredible double mystery—how did a German computer expert steal top secret information, and who killed him?

Fifty years ago, the world's first electronic computer weighed more than 33 tons and needed a building to house it. Now computers weigh just a few ounces and are pocket-size. While everyone expected computers to become smaller and faster, few envisioned a worldwide network of computers linked by telephone cables—the Internet. Or even more astonishing perhaps, the fact that files can be exchanged, globally, in a matter of seconds.

However, this new technology, with all its promise of a bright future, has also revealed the darker side of human nature. First came computer viruses, bugs introduced by mischief-makers, that are capable of causing havoc on computer systems worldwide. Then came a new kind of burglar. This crafty newcomer doesn't break into your home to rifle through your precious belongings. Nor does he loiter in the shadows, waiting to pounce on you as you walk the streets at night. Instead, from the comfort of his own home, he enters the computer files of people next door, or thousands of miles away, and plunders valued possessions.

This is the tale of a group of such thieves. A collection of individuals who hold the dubious distinction of being pioneers of computer pillage. They struck at a time when humankind was still wide-eyed about the dazzling new technology. But their actions ensured that people would forever be aware of the more sinister uses of that technology and the need to protect their most important files.

Files marked:

CHAPTER ONE

I ran. I ran as fast as my legs could carry me. Panting and gasping, I elbowed my way roughly through the crowds of Christmas shoppers, ignoring their grunts and curses. I didn't know where I was going. I just ran.

The icy winter winds burned my face, and my left ear still throbbed from where the Rhino had clouted me with his shovel-like hand. Through the pain I imagined I could still hear his booming voice mocking me and could still see the terrified eyes of poor, harmless Karl Muller, staring at him like a rabbit caught in the headlights of a car. On and on I ran, losing myself in the hordes of festive shoppers. Trying to become just another face in the crowd. But always looking over my shoulder, just in case. In case I was being followed.

At last, exhausted, I slowed to a walk. It was dark, and the snow drifts were more than three feet high when I realized that by some miracle my aimless wanderings had led me home. Here and there a carrot-nosed snowman stood in frozen silence as I trudged through the crisp, white blanket of snow. The streetlights illuminated the pathway to my house, where the cheerful lights of our Christmas tree shone through the window like a beacon of normality. Somehow I managed to fend off my parents' questions. My lungs were still aching as I climbed the stairs and sank wearily into my bed. I didn't know then that I would never see Karl again.

For a few minutes I lay curled up in the dark, feeling only relief that I was safe at last. Outside, big snowflakes floated noiselessly past my bedroom window. Then the tears began to trickle down my face as the voices inside my head returned. It seemed a lifetime ago, but in reality I had known Karl Muller for only six months. In that short time I had seen him just a few times. And yet so much had happened; my life had changed in so many ways that I felt ten years older.

Hugging my knees as I waited for the shivers to subside, I thought back to the first time that I heard his voice.

"Hey, kid! Want to make some money?"

Suddenly it was warm again. The sun was blazing through the windows of The Friendly Café, and I was wearing my favorite T-shirt—the one with the leopard on the front.

"Are you *deaf*? I asked if you wanted to make some money."

The voice came from a table behind me. I swung around and nearly burst into a fit of giggles when I saw its owner. Hiding behind a pair of round, mirror-lens sunglasses was one of the strangest-looking people I had ever seen. He could only have been in his mid-twenties, I guessed—a shock of stringy, thinning hair made him look older, but the clusters of pimples around his mouth and on his forehead gave away his youth. He wore a white T-shirt, on which was printed the legend: No one gets out of here alive.

"How much?" I asked.

The stranger turned to his companion, a sallow, unshaven youth with an irritated look on his face, who was sitting across the table from him. He was wearing a pea jacket.

"How much?" the first speaker shrugged.

His angry-looking friend cleared his throat. "What do I care! A million marks! A thousand pounds! Ten billion dollars! Use your common sense!"

"Don't take less than 20 marks," whispered Willie Braun, who before this interruption had been sitting at my table, drinking soda and moaning about his older brother.

"Keep out of it, boy!" hissed the second man with the furious expression.

"No need to shout, Helmut." His friend spoke quietly.

"How many times do I have to tell you not to use my name in public!" snapped Helmut.

"Sorry."

"Twenty marks—depending on what it is you want me to do," I butted in.

"Fifteen," said the first man, turning to face me again.

"Seventeen."

"Fifteen, and that's my final offer. Take it or leave it." The stranger waited for a reply.

From the corner of my eye I could see Willie shuffling in his seat. I knew his game. Any moment now he was going to muscle in and offer to do the job for less than 15 marks.

"Okay—it's a deal!" I agreed. "What do I have to do?"

A crooked smile appeared on the stranger's face as he fished inside the pocket of his coat and pulled out the stub of a pencil and some paper. Licking the tip of the pencil, he rapidly scrawled some words and handed the paper to me.

"Go to this address," he told me, "and ask for 'Beagle.' Tell him Karl—that's me—sent you."

"Then what?" I shrugged.

"Beagle will give you a package," Karl continued. He produced another piece of paper and scribbled a few more lines on it. "Take it to this address—that's where I live—and you'll get your money."

"Sounds easy enough to me," I said suspiciously. "What's stopping you from doing it yourself?"

"None of your business!" snarled Helmut, slamming his clenched fist down on the table and almost overturning his friend's coffee mug.

"Do you want to make this money or not?" asked Karl.

I did. So without asking any more questions, I stuffed the piece of paper into the back pocket of my jeans and set off. I knew I'd have no trouble finding the place—it was in an area of town that I knew quite well; a shopping mall on the outskirts of Hanover that was sometimes used by skateboarders. As I walked, I began to plan how I was going to spend the money. I was there in fifteen minutes.

"Seven Dortmund Strasse," I mumbled to myself, feeling rather pleased with the morning's turn of events.

The store I was standing in front of appeared to be totally deserted. It was sandwiched between a jewelry store and a bakery. There was no sign, and the window was blanked out and covered in layers of old posters. I gave the door a push.

It was locked, but I noticed a bell to one side. I tried it. There was no reply. I rang a second and then a third time and had just about given up hope of getting any answer when suddenly I heard a faint sound of movement from within. Then there was a sound of someone fumbling with the door lock. With a creak, the door slowly swung open, and a tiny, hunched old woman stepped stiffly out into the hazy sunshine. Her curly hair was as white as the cotton apron she wore. She must have been at least a hundred years old. After a moment, she removed the cigarette from between her lips and asked, "Yes, who is it?"

"Er—I've come to see Beagle," I replied hesitantly.

"Beagle?" said the old woman. "What are you talking about?"

"I was told to come to this address and pick up a package from Beagle."

With a look of disapproval on her face, the old woman sighed and slowly turned back into the store. In a wispy, high-pitched voice she called out to someone:

"Wilheim! Wilheim! Get your lazy, fat behind down here!"

Once again she moved slowly out from the darkness of the store. "You'd better come in and see my husband," she said, squinting into the sunlight. "Be careful you don't break anything."

The interior of the store was a treasure trove. Beneath piles of dust, which could easily have been there since the storekeeper was a young girl, were box upon box of pencils, erasers, pens, crayons, Scotch tape, and paper. The store evidently belonged to a stationer.

There was a loud cough behind me. Then I felt a tap on my shoulder.

"Seen two wars this store has," proclaimed a weary male voice. "Seen people rise, seen people fall flat on their faces."

Turning around, I got my first look at the owner of the voice. Like his wife, he was ancient. He had one of those faces that seems to have outgrown itself. Each of his withered features was somehow too big. The ears hung like pieces of puffy, unbaked dough beneath mottled sideburns.

4

The cracked and wrinkled lips seemed larger than they had any right to be. The nose, knotty and gnarled as an old oak tree, supported a pair of glasses that looked distinctly ill at ease on their precarious perch. Suddenly it hit me, and I put my hand over my mouth to stop myself from laughing—he looked like a beagle!

"There's been seven generations of us in this store," the old man continued with a hint of sadness. "We've watched this country rise to greatness only to be split in two."

"Oh, shut up you old fool," interrupted his wife, sourly. "Serve the young fellow—he hasn't got time to listen to you rambling on about the past!"

A frown appeared on the storekeeper's forehead as he shuffled toward me. "What is it you want then, sonny? Coloring books? Pencils? We've got everything here! Perhaps you'd like a good quality..."

"Be quiet," cut in his wife before he had time to finish the sentence, "let him speak!"

"I was sent by Karl Muller to pick up a package," I mumbled.

Instantly, the old man's face clouded. "Oh—him!" he snapped. "Young fool!"

"Go and get the parcel!" demanded his wife.

Grumbling to himself as he went, the storekeeper slowly disappeared into a little room at the back of the store. I gave the old woman a nervous smile.

"What was it you called him earlier?" she asked.

"I beg your pardon?"

"Earlier on, you called him a name."

"I think it was Beagle," I answered quietly.

"Speak up! My ears aren't what they used to be, you know."

I could see the storekeeper emerging from the back room clutching a parcel wrapped in brown paper.

"Beagle," I said loudly and clearly. "It was Beagle."

The old woman's face split into a delighted grin. "Beagle! Very funny!" she cackled. "I like that—Beagle!"

The storekeeper scowled as he handed the parcel to me

along with a slip of paper. "Give this to Muller," he instructed. "He'll know what it's for."

"Beagle!" repeated his wife. "Very amusing!"

With the politest thank you I could muster, I hurried from the dark and dusty store out into the brilliant sunshine. Taking a gulp of clean air I headed off toward Karl Muller's address. I could still hear the old woman's laughter as I crossed the street.

CHAPTER TWO

"How did the old guy like his nickname?" Karl Muller smirked at me from behind his sunglasses as he led me up a flight of stairs to his apartment.

"You mean you did that on purpose?" I gasped. "Very funny!"

"Just my little joke," he sniggered.

Karl's apartment was located beneath a hair salon in a part of town that my parents would have described as being "off the beaten track." It wasn't a pleasant area. The people on the streets were ashen-faced, poorly dressed, sad-looking men and women with menace in their eyes. They looked at me as if I had no right to be there. They made me feel uncomfortable.

The apartment itself wasn't a pretty sight either. You got the impression that Karl wasn't really one for entertaining. Judging from the state of his living room, he preferred his own company. Piles of old newspapers, magazines, and dog-eared, yellowing paper spilled over the frayed cushions of the cheap furniture. Coffee cups with mold crawling over the rims stood beside dirty ashtrays, overflowing with cigarette butts. "It's not much, but I call it home," announced Karl. "Take a seat and I'll get you something to drink."

While he left the room to make some coffee, I took another look at my surroundings. It really was a mess. Squalid. *Filthy.* Yet strangely enough there was one corner of the apartment that was meticulously clean. Beneath a window was a shiny wooden desk that, surprisingly, smelled of fresh polish. And sitting on top of the desk was a computer.

"She's a beauty, isn't she," breathed a voice behind me. Karl Muller had reentered the room carrying two steaming mugs of coffee. "Two megabytes of RAM. Eighty megabyte hard disk. Twelve hundred baud modem. A beauty!"

"It's a computer, is it?" I asked.

"Oh, it's a computer all right," sighed Karl.

"What's it for?"

"What's it for?" echoed Karl, raising his voice. "It's my window to the world, that's what it's for!"

I looked at him, puzzled, as he continued.

"From the keyboard of this computer I can travel to any place on this planet. I can talk to people I will never meet in my lifetime. I can visit places that you could only dream about. Cool, huh?" His voice bubbled with enthusiasm. He raked a hand through his stringy hair. I watched him become animated for the first time.

Karl moved over to the desk and pushed a button at the front of the computer, which was cream-colored and shaped like a pizza box. There was a "ping" as the machine ground slowly into action. "Come closer," he urged. "Come and take a look."

He flicked another switch, this time on the front of a monitor that looked like a TV screen sitting beside the computer. The screen flickered into life. "Now for my modem," he said, depressing a third switch, this time located on a small square object sitting at the other side of the computer.

"Ever used a computer?" asked Karl.

I shook my head.

"See those figures?" he enthused, pointing at the seemingly random series of numbers and letters that filled the screen. "They're telling us that the computer's system is booting up. The system tells the computer what to do."

I shrugged my shoulders. What he was saying meant nothing to me. I was getting bored. "Got any games?" I asked.

"Oh, I've got better stuff than that," declared Karl, as the machine gave another "ping." He began furiously tapping at the keyboard. "Name a place."

"Pardon?"

"Name a place. Go on—name a place anywhere in the world."

"What for?"

"Just do it!" he grinned, waving his hands enthusiastically in the air.

"Okay," I shrugged. I thought for a moment. "China?"

"China it is then!" Karl announced briskly.

He turned back to the screen and a look of concentration spread over his face. For the next few minutes he bent over the keyboard, typing in a complicated series of instructions. "First of all," he said as he worked, "we'll take a little trip to Hamburg."

As I watched, a message appeared on the screen. Stooping over Karl's shoulder I could just about make out some of it. "WELCOME TO HAMBURG RESOURCE LABORATORIES. PLEASE TYPE IN YOUR PASSWORD" it read.

Karl's fingers scampered quickly over the keyboard as he spoke again, "Now how about a visit to New York City?"

My eyes widened as once again a message came onto the screen. I could only understand one or two words; however, it was evidently no problem for Karl, who swiftly typed a response.

"And now," announced my companion with a note of drama in his voice, "let's move on to Peking!" As he spoke, a third message appeared on the computer screen. The words were written in Chinese script.

He looked up at me. The triumph on his face quickly turned to disappointment as he noticed the bored expression on mine. "Yeah—cool," I said, trying to sound more enthusiastic than I felt. "What about some games?"

Karl lit a cigarette. He leaned back in his chair and stared at me. "How old are you?" he asked, after a minute.

"Fifteen," I lied, dropping my voice and adding an extra two years to my age. "Why?"

"It's just that people of your generation seem to think of nothing but games. You completely miss the fantastic possibilities that a box of tricks like this has to offer."

I could see that Karl was becoming frustrated by the fact that I didn't share his enthusiasm for the computer. I was beginning to wonder if he was ever going to pay me my money for picking up the parcel. All I wanted was to take it and go. But Karl obviously had other ideas.

"Take a look at this!" he urged.

For the next half an hour or so, Karl took me on a guided tour of his computer. The screen became a blur as he showed me a wealth of programs. Some were for designing pages, other allowed you to draw and paint, some even allowed you to make music. Karl glowed with pride as he boasted about the capabilities of his machine. I could see it was clever, but it just didn't fascinate me the way it did Karl.

My host seemed to lose track of time when he was sitting in front of his computer. But my stomach, which was starting to rumble, told me that it was time to get a move on.

"Look, I don't want to be a bore," I ventured, "but I'm really going to have to go home soon."

Karl turned away from his computer and looked into my eyes. I could see that he simply couldn't comprehend my lack of interest. He seemed to be taking my indifference as a personal slight. "I'll tell you what," he announced suddenly, "I'll show you something that *will* amaze you. Then you can leave."

I shrugged and offered a weak smile.

Karl moved so close to me that I could smell his breath. It smelled of a mixture of tobacco smoke and something else equally unhealthy. "Can you keep a secret?" he whispered.

"Depends," I replied, cautiously.

He glanced nervously around the room. "I'm going to show you something now that you must never tell anyone about. I'm not supposed to do this but, to be honest, kid, I've taken quite a shine to you."

"Okay," I shrugged. "What is it?" Whatever it was, I hoped it would be quick.

He turned his attention once more to the keyboard.

I looked on apathetically as Karl began to type in more commands. Again, what I was seeing on the screen made little sense to me. "Do you know what they call what I'm doing?" he asked, confidentially.

"'Fraid not," came my monotone response. Right then watching paint dry would have been more interesting than attempting to come up with an answer to Karl's question.

"It's called hacking."

"Hacking?" I said dryly. "Means nothing to me."

"You've never heard of hacking? You haven't lived! It's an art form that those of only sheer genius can indulge in," Karl declared—somewhat immodestly, I thought.

"You mean like painting and sculpture?"

"That's right," he continued excitedly, "except that I don't intend to starve for my art."

"What exactly is it then?" I repeated, looking at my watch.

"Oh, you can do all sorts of clever and useful things if you're a hacker."

"Like what?"

"Like lots of things."

"Like *what?*" I repeated once more.

Karl lowered his voice. "If you can hack you can take a journey on your modem to anywhere in the world."

"So?"

"So you can take a look at what's there."

I hesitated. The phrase "big deal" was on the tip of my tongue, and I had to swallow hard to stop myself from saying it.

Karl sounded exasperated now. "You simply don't realize the implications of this, do you?"

"Sorry," I said in a tired voice.

"If you only knew what I was doing now, for instance, you'd be amazed."

Enough was enough. I decided that I couldn't take any more of Karl and his cryptic games. All I wanted was for him to hurry up and pay me so I could leave. I got to my feet and began to fidget, trying to attract his attention. But Karl took no notice.

"That's interesting," he muttered, his voice becoming noticeably more serious.

I cast a longing glance toward the door of the shabby apartment and gave a loud cough.

Suddenly, Karl leaned forward, close to the computer screen. It was almost as if he wanted to shield the screen from my gaze—as if he didn't want me to see what was was on it.

"What's up?" I asked, slowly edging forward so that I was looking over his shoulder at the screen.

He didn't answer. He seemed to be in a trance, his gaze fixed firmly on the green light that emanated from the computer monitor. I followed the line of his vision and was surprised to see that among the gaggle of unintelligible gibberish that filled the screen were three letters that I had seen before. With creased forehead, I read them aloud.

"CIA."

Karl whirled around to face me. "Sshhhh!" he demanded. "Keep your voice down—you never know who's listening."

"Calm down," I urged, embarrassed at my host's sudden show of emotion.

Without warning, Karl jumped to his feet, hunched over the computer keyboard and began typing furiously. The computer screen went blank. I guessed that he had turned it off.

"Time you were leaving," he announced as the computer fell silent.

"But it was just getting interesting!" I protested.

Karl waved a finger in the air and shook his head. "I think you've seen quite enough," he said firmly.

This time it was my turn to shake my head. It was obvious that this strange person was trying to impress me. But why did he have to be so theatrical about it? It was irritating to say the least.

Once he was away from the computer, Karl seemed to return to his normal self. He smiled, rubbing his hands together. "Right," he said. "It's time you were paid for your afternoon's work."

He picked up the package I had brought to him, tore it open and inspected the contents—a sheaf of computer printouts. Karl ran his index finger down the figures on the top page and gave a satisfied grunt.

"You look as if you could do with earning some extra money," he said, turning to face me.

I nodded in agreement.

"Tell you what," he continued, "I'm often too busy at the computer to go out and pick up packages like the one you got today. Give me your address and phone number and I'll get in touch when I need you again."

He handed me a piece of paper and a pen and watched as I wrote down my details.

It was with some relief that I left the apartment and headed home. It felt as if I'd been in that place for weeks. I'd heard about types like Karl before—nuts who live, eat, and breathe computers. I wouldn't want him to start thinking of me as his friend. On the other hand, I reflected, a little extra money couldn't hurt. And if today's errand was anything to go by, what easier way of making cash could there be?

CHAPTER THREE

Hans Schmidt was bigger than me, but they told me he was slower. They were wrong. Our bout of after-school fistfights had left me with the salty taste of blood in my mouth and an ugly swelling above my right eye. The whole school had gathered at the gates to watch my classmate and me settle our argument by violence. Now, as I hung my head and began the long walk home, I wished I'd chosen to use words.

A month had passed since that strange afternoon spent in the company of Karl Muller. In that month I had been back to see Beagle and his ancient spouse on two occasions. All I had to do was pick up a small parcel and deliver it to Karl Muller's apartment. Both times there had been no reply when I knocked on Karl's door. At first I was worried that I wouldn't get paid for my troubles. However, a couple of days later a letter had arrived at my house containing two crisp bills.

Although it crossed my mind that it was strange that Karl never seemed to be home, I didn't waste time worrying about it. I had other things on my mind. The main priority was, as always, school. School and parents. Somehow the two were inexorably linked. If I didn't perform well at school there was always the threat of a letter to my parents. If there was something I did at home that my parents didn't like, it had to be due to a problem at school. I just couldn't win.

And there was no doubt at all that I wasn't going to win tonight. I had a grim premonition that the battering I'd received from my overweight schoolmate Hans Schmidt was nothing compared to the one that was waiting for me at home when my father caught sight of me. It wasn't only the cuts and bruises; there was also the little matter of the rip in the knee of my best school pants—a gaping hole that seemed to get bigger the longer I looked at it.

Added to my misery was the thought of going back to

school on Monday morning, seeing the mocking faces of my schoolmates, and hearing their sniggers. The whole school had seen me get beaten to a pulp by Schmidt, and in our school, losers are given a hard time.

As the summer sun began to dip below the horizon, I trudged miserably homeward with downcast eyes.

"Been in the wars?"

For a moment it didn't register that someone was talking to me—I had been too busy avoiding the eyes of passersby. Now, I looked up and saw the face of Karl Muller. He stood in front of me smoking a cigarette and wearing a T-shirt that said: *This is the end.* It seemed an appropriate message considering my situation. He was still wearing those familiar mirror-lens sunglasses.

"Hello Karl," I muttered, not really knowing what else to say.

"What happened to you?" he asked. "Lose an argument with a bus?"

"Very funny," I said grimly.

I felt his hand on my shoulder. "Cheer up," he smiled. "Hop in my car and let me buy you a cup of coffee."

It was an offer I couldn't refuse. Karl seemed genuinely concerned, and besides, I would have done anything to delay going home.

He led me to his car. I had expected to see an old wreck, but to my surprise, there in front of me was a big, red two-seater gleaming in the last rays of sunshine. It seemed strangely out of character with the slightly grungy impression that Karl had made on me during our first encounter.

"Wow! Nice car," I exclaimed in admiration.

"Think so?" replied Karl, proudly.

I settled into the passenger's seat and tried to relax as he maneuvered the car through town. The interior of the sleek vehicle didn't match its shiny façade. Old, crumpled cigarette packs and newspapers lay scattered around on the floor in a manner that reminded me of Karl's apartment.

"You should get yourself a cleaner if you can afford a car

like this," I suggested.

"I'll get myself a cleaner if you get yourself a bodyguard," said Karl. He glanced at my cut face and winced. "Have you been fighting?"

We glided through the streets, and I gloomily recounted the chain of events that had led to my public humiliation at the hands of the school bully. Karl said little but nodded in sympathy as I talked. I was grateful for his company. By the time we reached the café where we had first met, I was starting to feel a little better about life.

Inside The Friendly Café, Karl bought me a cup of hot chocolate. It didn't soothe my injuries but it enlivened my spirits quite a bit.

"Actually, I'm glad I bumped into you," said Karl, after I had finished my sad tale.

"Oh?" I said.

"Yes," continued Karl. "I wanted to thank you for doing those little errands for me."

"No problem," was my reply. "But I'm afraid I won't have time to do any more in the near future—I'm getting really bogged down with my homework."

"You should get yourself a computer," said my companion. "You'll whizz through your homework."

I snorted. "And how would I pay for it?"

"It would pay for itself in no time," Karl advised. "Mine has!"

"Anyway, I wouldn't know what to do with it."

Karl folded his arms and leaned forward. "Listen," he said, lowering his voice, "why don't we go back to my apartment? You can clean yourself up and I'll dig out a needle and thread for that hole in your pants."

I thought about it for a moment, then shrugged, "Okay." Anything was better than going home to face the music.

Karl took a furtive look around the café. It was empty except for a couple of scruffily dressed men, one of whom was wearing a flatcap and quietly smoking a pipe. He winked conspiratorially.

"I'll even let you fool around with my computer!"

The first thing that hit me when we arrived at my companion's apartment was the smell. It stank of rancid food and stale tobacco. The source of this vile odor seemed to be several plates of half-eaten food that had been discarded around the living room. They were dotted with cigarette butts and crawling with silverfish. Even Karl seemed a little shamefaced about the mess as he guided me toward the small oasis of hygiene that was his shrine to the digital age.

I had been glad enough to sit with Karl and pour out my tale of woe, but I had sensed all along that he had an ulterior motive in inviting me over to his apartment. And sure enough, it wasn't long before he was sitting in front of his computer with the green light of its screen illuminating his eager face. "Now then, I seem to remember the last time we met that I took you on a small trip on the Internet," he said brightly. "Care to take another journey?"

"There's no need," I replied, my mind still occupied with thoughts of what would happen to me when I returned home.

"Oh, yes there is," Karl said, trying to cheer me up. "I'm making it my personal responsibility to bring a smile to your miserable face."

"Well, watching you play with a computer is the last thing I need," I muttered bitterly.

"You may scoff," grinned Karl, "but you might find that sooner or later you'll change your attitude."

As I dabbed at my cuts and bruises with the washcloth that Karl had given me, I watched his frantic fingers dance across the keyboard. "Let's see how a bit of foreign travel will cheer you up," he announced excitedly.

As before, the computer screen filled up with unreadable gibberish. "Here's our first stop," Karl exclaimed. "A brief visit to sunny Hamburg."

Sure enough, the words on the screen began to make a little sense. They were written in German and invited the user to enter a password. Karl tapped a few more keys and waited for a moment. "That's funny," he exclaimed. "I must have mistyped."

He typed some more.

A look of irritation appeared on his face. "Someone seems to have changed my password!"

His words meant nothing to me. I held the cloth to my swollen eye.

"What do you do if the front door's locked?" asked Karl enigmatically, turning to face me.

I gave a noncommittal shrug of my shoulders.

"You go in through the back door, that's what you do!" he cried, and attacked the keyboard with renewed vigor.

A new message appeared on the screen. "WELCOME TO BERKELEY LABORATORIES. AWAITING INSTRUCTIONS."

"Eureka!" Karl cried, a smile lighting up his face. "They think they're clever, but they don't know who they're dealing with!"

I got the distinct feeling that he was trying to impress me again.

"Now then, let's go surfing in California," he said, his words accompanied by another burst of typing. "Let's see what's up."

After a five-second wait the words on the computer screen turned into English. Like a man possessed, Karl began to type with even more vigor. From beneath those sunglasses, something had obviously caught his eye. "Interesting," he confirmed, picking up a notebook that was lying on the floor beneath the desk, "SDINET—I've never noticed that before."

For the first time, I found myself beginning to get interested in whatever my host was doing as he furiously hammered away at the keyboard. Maybe his enthusiasm was finally rubbing off on me.

Suddenly Karl bent forward, closed his eyes, and rested his forehead in the palms of his hands. He stayed like that for a moment or two, and when he raised his head his expression was triumphant. "Gold," he said simply. He held out a hand for me to shake.

I hesitated before reluctantly taking it. I had expected it to be cold and clammy; and I was right.

"I've just struck gold," he announced.

"Congratulations." I smiled, again not knowing what on earth he was talking about.

"Look, you've got to leave now," said Karl, getting to his feet. "I don't mean to be rude but I've got work to do."

As he spoke, my eyes were drawn toward the computer screen. Amid the jumble of green letters that cast an eerie glow over the apartment were two words that I recognized instantly: TOP SECRET I frowned as I scanned these two words. Top Secret?

"You're becoming my lucky mascot," said Karl, who had noticed the puzzled expression on my face.

"I beg your pardon?"

Karl cleared his throat and positioned himself in front of the computer screen so that its contents were obscured. "You've only been here twice," he explained, "and both times you've brought me good luck."

"What do you mean?"

"Can't explain right now," said Karl. "Some other time, perhaps."

"But why don't you tell me what is it that you've discovered?" I demanded. "I'd really like to know. I wasn't interested at first, but I am now—honest!"

"Look, I haven't got time to answer questions now—later, maybe," said Karl, ignoring my protests. "Take a taxi home."

Before my astonished eyes he reached into his pocket and pulled out a huge roll of money. He peeled off a ten deutsche mark bill and handed it to me.

"Tell nobody—and I *mean* nobody—about what you've seen," Karl instructed me in a serious voice. "I mean it. It's important."

Then he seemed to relax again. "And I hope your bruises get better. You're going to have quite a shiner tomorrow!"

CHAPTER FOUR

Karl wasn't wrong. When I awoke the next morning and stared glumly into the bathroom mirror, I saw the face of another person gazing back at me. Someone who looked like he'd gone 15 rounds with a champion heavyweight boxer. My right eye was tightly closed and surrounded by an ugly circle of blue and yellow bruising. I shook my head at the grisly sight.

As expected, I'd received no sympathy from my parents. Instead, they'd given me a lecture on teenage violence and a temporary reduction of my allowance. I suppose it could have been worse—at least I'd managed to conceal the damage to my school pants. If it hadn't been for Karl's timely intervention, I might have spent what remained of the summer staring at the ceiling of my bedroom. It seems funny looking back, because as the year drew to a close, there were times when I wished I was doing just that.

I'd had a fitful night's sleep. Somehow, I couldn't get Karl, his computer and the words "TOP SECRET" out of my mind. All of a sudden, the world of computers seemed mysterious and fascinating. What was this strange man doing? How could he live in such filth and yet afford to own an expensive sports car? What exactly was he up to?

There was only one thing to do: I decided I'd try to find out.

That lunchtime, I paid a visit to the school library and browsed through a stack of books about computers. Most of them were just boring technical manuals, but I found one about a subject I had heard Karl mention in his apartment. Something called the Internet. Skimming through the pages of the book, I began to understand a little about what Karl was doing. Using a modem, which was the small box-shaped object that sat next to his computer and made a strange whistling noise, Karl was "logging on" to a worldwide network of computers that made up this thing called the Internet. According to the book, once logged on to the Internet, it was possible to go to any place in the world that also had a computer connected to it. In this way, files and information could be freely exchanged.

It seemed simple enough—but Karl implied that he was making money out of his travels. I could find no mention of how to do that. I put the book in my backpack, planning to have a more in-depth look later on.

I spent most of that afternoon sitting in the back of the classroom looking at my wristwatch. I couldn't concentrate on anything as mundane as schoolwork. My thoughts kept returning to the Internet. I was also trying to ignore the stares and whispers of my classmates. It would be a long time before they forgot yesterday's humiliating defeat. When it was finally time to go home I left before any of them had the opportunity to make any wisecracks to my face. Keeping my eyes low, I strode out through the school gates and headed off in the direction of Karl's apartment. I had a lot of questions to ask him.

Scarcely out of breath, I reached Karl's place in under 30 minutes and rang the doorbell. When there was no response I tried again. For a minute I thought I heard slight sounds of movement from within, but still there was no answer. Suddenly, just as I was beginning to reconcile myself to a long trek home, I felt a powerful hand clamp down on my shoulder. There was a sudden pungent smell of tobacco smoke as a second hand wrapped itself tightly around my mouth. Unable to cry out and too shocked to react, I found myself hoisted off my feet and dragged into a nearby car.

The sound of the vehicle's engine throbbed in my ears as, shaking with fear, I tried to take in what was happening to me. I made a futile attempt to struggle free, but it was no use —my kidnapper was far too strong. His rough hands held me firmly, and all I could do was twist my head and try to get a look at him. Shabbily dressed and wearing a flat canvas cap, he must have been in his late forties. His features weren't so much aged as eroded, like an old cliff. A network of lines was etched deep into a forehead that looked like it had been chiseled out of granite. A wide, snub nose, set beneath a pair of watery eyes only served to accentuate the general aura of nastiness that hung around him. Noticing that I had stopped struggling, my captor released his grip from around my mouth and silently raised a finger to his rubbery lips in a warning to keep quiet. As the car raced through the streets driven by his silent companion, I felt it would be unwise to ignore that warning.

Powerless, I looked on in terror as the monster sitting beside me pulled open my backpack. His hands looked like concrete as he rifled though its contents. When he discovered the book on the Internet he shot me a glance of pure hatred.

I turned away and tried to get a glimpse of the other man, who was sitting with his back to me in the driver's seat. His features, however, were obscured. All I could see was his bald head and the reflection of my terrified face in the rear view mirror. Finally, I could take no more and had to speak. "Who are you?" I said in a trembling voice.

The brute beside me gave my shoulder a push with the back of his hand and once more signaled to me to be silent. Unwilling to risk rousing his anger, I sat in miserable silence and watched the sights of the city go by. As we traveled, it suddenly dawned on me that the two men seemed slightly familiar. I began to study them, all the time becoming more and more convinced that I had seen them before. Then I remembered where. They had been sitting in The Friendly Café last night when I had been there with Karl.

The trip seemed to go on for hours, then at last the car began to decelerate as we reached an industrial park far from the center of town. We pulled up beside a deserted warehouse, and I was hustled out of the car and pushed toward a door. Our footsteps echoed as we stepped through a cloud of dust into a veil of half-light.

"Please sit down," ordered the driver of the car.

I looked around me. The interior of the warehouse was completely empty except for three chairs and a small table.

Without a word I did as he said.

"You must be wondering why we've brought you here," he continued as I eyed him suspiciously. It was my first chance to have a good look at him. He was distinctly less threatening than his companion—not that that made me feel any better. Short of stature and quite lightly built, he had a face that was *almost* friendly. Almost—but not quite. His lack of hair gave him a demonic appearance that was heightened by the angular eyebrows that sliced across his face. You almost expected to see two horns poking through what was left of his hairline.

Now the man who had been beside me in the car spoke:

"I'm going to be brief," he announced in a voice that could curdle milk. "I expect you to cooperate. I don't intend to hang around."

I watched miserably as he produced a pipe from his coat pocket and began to fill it with tobacco. "Some people call me the Rhino," he growled. "My real name needn't concern you. Just answer my questions and nothing bad will happen to you."

"What do you want to know?" I asked. I tried to sound calm, but the tremble in my voice betrayed my fear.

The Rhino sniffed and then spoke: "Twice you have been seen entering the apartment of Karl Muller. When we picked you up this evening you had been seen attempting to enter that dirt-hole of an apartment of his for the third time. Exactly what is your relationship with him? Please tell."

"I've only known him a short time," I replied quickly. "He's just someone I met in a café."

"Would that be The Friendly Café?" said the other man, a thin smile creeping over his lips.

"That's right," I said. "Is Karl in some kind of trouble?"

I jumped as, without warning, the Rhino's fist slammed down hard on the table. "I'll ask the questions!" he bellowed. Then, just as suddenly, he was calm again. He lowered himself into the chair next to mine. "What do you know about Karl Muller?"

I shook my head in puzzlement. "He's just someone I met

23

in a café," I repeated.

The Rhino finished packing his pipe with brown tobacco and pushed it into the bowl with a stained thumb. "I will say it once more: What is your relationship with Karl Muller?"

I shrugged my shoulders. There was nothing more I could tell him.

My tormentor produced a lighter, flicked it on, and cupped his hand around the naked flame. He glared at me menacingly.

"Look, I really don't know anything about Karl Muller! I'm telling the truth!" My voice was a mere whimper now.

Slowly, methodically, the Rhino raised his pipe to his lips and applied the flame to its bowl. The sweet smell of burning tobacco drifted toward me as he sucked at the stem of the pipe and gave a satisfied grunt. "You're lying," he said simply.

It was then that the other man leaned over and whispered something into his companion's ear. As he listened, the Rhino never took his eyes off me. He greeted his comrade's words with an occasional nod of his head as I strained to hear what was being said. After a few moments he rose from his chair and left the warehouse, slamming the door behind him.

"Don't mind my friend," said the other man, the false smile returning to his face. "He's just a little bad-tempered sometimes."

"What do you want from me?" I asked nervously.

"Not a lot," said the other man. "Just some information and we'll take you home."

"What sort of information?"

The man's smile broadened, revealing an uneven set of stained teeth. "Just tell me what you know about Karl Muller."

I rubbed my eyes. "I told you before: he's someone I met in a café. What has he done?"

"That's not your problem."

"Well, I can't tell you anything," I insisted, fidgeting in my chair.

My questioner perched himself on the still-warm chair that had recently been vacated by the Rhino. "Listen," he said softly, "between you and me, I don't like this job. My friend out there, he likes the job even less—and when he's angry he's no fun to be around."

"What is your job?" I inquired.

Leaning forward on his elbows, my inquisitor lowered his voice and, for the second time in a month, I heard the words: "Can you keep a secret?"

I nodded.

"I've been asked to find out what I can about Muller," he continued. "Keep it under your hat."

"But *why* do you want to know about Karl?"

"Because the people who tell me what to do suspect that he's been a naughty boy."

Without warning, the door to the warehouse swung open, and the menacing silhouette of the Rhino filled the doorway. His partner moved to meet him and once again a lengthy whispered discussion ensued.

"But what about the book he was carrying!" I heard the Rhino snarl.

"It's a coincidence," said the other man. "He's only a kid—he knows nothing."

After a while the voices died down and the Rhino stomped over to me. "You can go now," he said, making a gesture toward the door, "but be careful." His gaze fixed on the knot of swelling above my eye. "If I find out you've been lying to me you'll have more problems than a black eye!"

CHAPTER FIVE

The center of the city was bathed in moonlight when my two captors finally allowed me to leave the car. My return journey from the warehouse had been even less enjoyable than the harrowing trip out. If I had any consolation at all it was that I didn't have to share the backseat with the hulking Rhino, who had chosen to sit in the front with his friend. Most of the trip was spent in silence. The few words that were spoken by my kidnappers were scarcely discernible, although once or twice I thought I heard them speaking English.

When the car eventually came to a stop, it was the Rhino himself who pulled open the car door and indicated with a jerk of his thumb that I was free to go. I jumped out into the street and immediately broke into a run, the shadows of the night stretching out around me. When I was sure the car must have pulled away, I risked a look back over my shoulder and saw its taillights receding into the far distance. It was then that I realized that I had been put out of the car at the very same place at which I had been picked up hours earlier. I was in sight of Karl Muller's apartment. Looking up at his window, I could see that a light was on.

Still trembling, I rang his bell. At first it seemed that he wasn't going to answer, but after a few moments the door opened a crack and I heard his familiar voice say, "What are you doing here?"

Karl's face was serious as he beckoned me inside. He was still wearing his round sunglasses, and the motto on his T-shirt now read: Mr. Mojo Rising. "What do you think you're doing?" he snapped. "You mustn't come here uninvited."

Hurriedly, I pushed my way past him. "I've got to talk to you," I said.

Inside Karl's apartment, I spilled out the whole story between sips of black coffee. As I spoke, Karl removed his glasses and stared at me intently. It was the first time I had seen him without glasses on, and there was real concern in his eyes.

He let me finish my story without interrupting. Only when I had been silent for a moment or two did he speak. "I'm sorry—really sorry—that this has happened to you," he said slowly. "It's all a terrible misunderstanding."

"Do you know those people?" I panted. My heart was still thumping.

"Not personally," Karl replied. "They're friends of Helmut."

"Helmut?"

"He was the guy I was sitting with in the café when I first met you."

Suddenly I remembered Helmut's irritated, angry face. "I don't understand," I said. "What's he got to do with all this?"

Karl lowered his voice and leaned toward me. "Those men you met are paying us money for a certain service that we provide," he explained. "They were just trying to protect their investment."

"What do you mean?" I frowned.

He moved over to his computer and motioned for me to join him. "I shouldn't really be telling you this, but it's out of my hands now," he said soberly. "Thanks to Helmut's idiot friends, you're involved."

"I don't understand."

"I'm not surprised," said Karl. "There's no reason at all why you should understand."

He reached into his jeans pocket and pulled out a pack of cigarettes. "Remember I once told you about hacking?" he said, lighting up.

"Yes," I nodded.

"Well, that's what I am—a *hacker*!" Even now he couldn't resist putting a hint of drama into his voice.

A thin gray ribbon of cigarette smoke curled into the air as he continued. "I make money by hacking into certain places and selling any information I find there to certain people I know."

"What sort of information?"

The expression on Karl's face changed. I had never seen him look so serious. "The best way to tell you is to show you," he said.

As I looked on, he began to tap away at his computer keyboard. Soon the screen was filled with the familiar lines of gibberish as the machine began to communicate with the Internet. Karl spoke quickly as his fingers skipped nimbly over the keyboard. "Listen carefully. What I'm doing now is contacting a secret computer base in Hamburg," he explained. "From here I am given a gateway to similar bases all over the world."

As he finished speaking, the words "TOP SECRET— PLEASE ENTER YOUR PASSWORD" appeared on the computer screen. They were written in English.

"What are you doing now?" I inquired breathlessly.

"I'm now entering a classified air base in the United States," he said calmly. "Let me just input the password."

"What's the password for?"

"The password permits entry into the base. If you know the password you are given direct access to all the top secret information stored in the base's computers."

"Such as?" I inquired.

"Such as anything that's available at these sites. Secret plans, blueprints, computer encryption systems, classified letters, and reports. You know the sort of stuff."

Whatever that sort of stuff was, it sounded important to me. "How do you know the password?" I asked.

Karl stopped typing and sat bolt upright. "Because people are so stupid," he announced, some of the arrogance back in his voice now. "Entering this air base should be impossible. The password should be completely foolproof."

"You still haven't told me *how*."

"Finding out a password is child's play," explained Karl, flicking the stub of his cigarette into an ashtray. "I've written a small program that does it for me. It took me only ten minutes to write, and it can guess almost any system password within hours."

I was impressed.

"Remember when you were here last time?" asked Karl.

"Of course."

"Then you might recall my telling you that I'd struck gold."

I nodded.

"And you probably thought I seemed a little excited?"

I nodded again.

"That was because in my travels on the Internet I'd discovered a batch of electronic mail in an air base in Berkeley. The papers related to a top secret project named SDINET."

"Go on!" I said excitedly, wanting to know more.

Karl sighed and gave me a long look. "You don't understand do you?"

I hesitated. "Sorry, I don't."

"Let me put it this way: who do you think pays for my nice new car?"

I shook my head.

"Okay, I'll put it even more simply," he continued. "But you must never—I repeat, *never*—tell anyone about this."

As if to heighten the suspense, Karl turned toward the keyboard and typed a few more words. There was a brief silence before he turned back to me. "I'm a spy," he said simply.

"A what?"

"A spy—and so's Helmut. We're paid by the KGB to steal top secret information from the Internet."

"You're kidding," I gasped. I wondered whether it was some kind of joke.

"It's true—I'm deadly serious," said Karl, and the look in his eyes convinced me he meant it. Despite his calm manner, it was noticeable that his revelations were uttered with a sense of pride.

"Isn't that against the law?" I asked.

"Of course it's against the law," Karl replied scornfully. "And that's the reason why we must never meet again."

He lit up another cigarette before continuing.

"You already know far too much for your own good. It's better that you go back to school and forget about everything you've seen here."

"But won't the police be after you?" I asked, my head spinning.

A wry smile returned to Karl's face. He was obviously getting some kind of thrill out of the situation. "I'll never be caught," he announced, with a hint of a swagger. "I'm too clever for all of 'em!"

I took a long look at Karl. He was nothing like James Bond, or any of the other spies in the movies. It was true that he had a flashy car, but that was about as far as it went. He didn't wear a tuxedo, there was no string of beautiful women at his beck and call. And unlike the spies in the movies, it was obvious that beneath Karl's boastful exterior he was frightened. Very frightened.

"How much do they pay you?" I asked.

Karl tutted and smiled. "That's for me to know and you never to find out," he laughed. "Anyway, I don't do it for the money."

"What do you do it for, then?" I frowned.

"Look, I'd be a liar if I said that the money didn't come in handy," he admitted. "But my real motivation is liberty—freedom of information. I believe there should be no secrets in this world, especially in computers."

"So you sell them to the KGB," I said cynically.

Karl thought for a moment before speaking. "Enough of this chatter," he said finally. "Now you must go. And remember, tell no one about this."

"Don't worry," I mumbled.

As Karl ushered me to the door he held out a limp, sweaty palm for me to shake. Slowly, I took it and held it in my own. Even though he was much older than I, Karl's hand was swallowed by mine. It was the hand of a child.

"Nice knowing you, kid," he said, pulling out his wad of money and handing me a crisp bill.

"Glad you think so," I replied.

"Take a taxi home and don't worry about any of this," he

said weakly. "I'll talk to Helmut. Those men will never bother you again."

I was halfway home before I began to realize that pieces of Karl's incredible story simply didn't fit together. If the two men who had picked me up in their car were from the KGB, why did they tell me they were investigating a *crime*? Why were they so interested in Karl Muller if he was already working for them? And why had I heard them speaking English? As the taxi headed for home, I wondered whether Karl had told me the whole story.

CHAPTER SIX

My bruises faded and so did the summer. The days grew shorter and darker, and as red and gold leaves began to pile up on the streets of Hanover, my memories of Karl Muller became little more than a dream. There were many times when I had to ask myself if it had all really happened. Had I really been in the—albeit brief—employ of a full-fledged Internet spy? Did I really get kidnapped by two members of the KGB? I couldn't even begin to separate truth from fantasy.

Indeed, Karl Muller and his magical modem would have become permanently consigned to history were it not for a letter I received one morning in late November. It came amid a stack of birthday cards that had been sent to me to celebrate my 14th birthday. Inside was a slip of blue-lined writing paper that contained just six words. Roughly scrawled in pencil they read: MEET ME AT THE CAFE. SATURDAY.

There was no indication of who the sender was, but somehow I knew where it had come from. I also had a hunch as to the location of the café it referred to. That's how it came about that I spent most of Saturday sitting at the window of The Friendly Café, patiently looking out for the disheveled form of Karl Muller. Karl, however, never showed up.

The place was empty, and its owner was sweeping away the day's cigarette butts when the mysterious letter writer finally turned up. He was wearing a sheepskin coat, the collar of which he clutched around his unshaven face—a face that was white with fear.

"Helmut!" I exclaimed in surprise.

He dipped his eyes and took hold of the sleeve of my coat. "Quick, out of here!" he said. "They're on to us!"

Helmut half pulled, half dragged me through the city

streets. We charged along as if our lives depended on it. Ignoring my breathless protests and continually looking over his shoulder, Helmut led me to his apartment. It was located down a side street not far from the city center. Once inside, it soon became evident that Helmut enjoyed his home comforts more than the slovenly Karl Muller.

Helmut's apartment was the proverbial palace. Newly decorated, and with a carpet you could have drowned in, the place reeked of money. All around me lay the trappings of success. A gleaming stereo, an enormous TV, and a collection of electronic gadgets whose purpose I could only guess at.

In the corner of the room sat a computer that was obviously several classes above the one I'd seen at Karl's place. It was bigger, and had a screen that was twice the size of Karl's.

Whatever Helmut did for a living, there was no doubt that he was highly successful at it—and it wasn't difficult to guess his means of employment. He sat me down in a plush, easy chair and spoke. "How much has he told you?" he asked.

I didn't know what he was talking about. "What do you mean?" I said.

"How much do you know about what we're doing?" he said. His face wore the same angry look that I had seen when we originally met. "How much has that imbecile Muller been telling you?"

"He told me a little bit about what he was doing," I answered, truthfully.

Helmut punched the air in fury. "I knew I couldn't trust that fool! Now we're all in danger and it's his fault!"

He slumped down in a chair opposite me and struggled out of his coat. It was only then that I realized how ill he looked. Without his coat he appeared seriously underweight. His skin had an unhealthy white pallor, and there was a curious, haunted look in his sunken eyes. Like Karl, he seemed to be very scared—and like Karl, he was making a very bad job of hiding his fear. "You're going to have to help," he said at last.

I didn't like the sound of that. "Me? What can I do?"

"They're watching Karl's apartment and they're following me—I'm sure of it!" Helmut explained. "The game's up if they see me go anywhere near Karl."

"Who's they?" I asked.

"The *FBI*, of course!"

"The *FBI*!" I exclaimed.

"Yes, the FBI!" Helmut repeated impatiently. "They've been following me for days. They know where Karl lives, and they intend to get us both!"

"But what can *I* do?" I protested.

Helmut gave a sharp intake of breath. "I just want you to warn him for me. You've got to go to his apartment and warn him."

There was an embarrassed silence as I tried to come up with an excuse. Then Helmut spoke again. This time there was an edge of despair in his voice.

"Everything's falling apart," he moaned. "I used to use that old idiot Beagle to pass my information to Karl. Now he won't answer his door."

My mind reeled. So that was what my errands to Beagle's store were all about! I was picking up orders from Helmut.

"Can't you call him?" I asked.

"Don't be stupid, boy," snapped an increasingly exasperated Helmut. "They're bound to have wire taps on both our lines!"

"Why not use the Internet?" I asked, quietly pleased with myself that I was able to put into action the knowledge I had gained from those computer manuals.

"Because I can't afford to take the chance. They can monitor my e-mail."

I hesitated for a moment.

"Sorry, but no thanks," I said.

My companion's angry glare had given way to an expression of panic. "Look, kid, if it's money you want I'll give you money—lots of it. Anything you want."

"I don't want any money."

"Do it for Karl then," pleaded Helmut. "You're friends now, aren't you? He's in great danger, too."

I looked down at my hands and saw that they were shaking. It was all getting far too serious. I wanted to go back to the safety of school and forget all about hacking, espionage, and stolen documents. I wanted to forget that I had ever heard of the KGB or the FBI. Most of all I wanted to be far away from the haggard, terrified figure of Helmut.

"I'm sorry," I repeated. "I'm going home."

Helmut's air of menace had changed to one of utter despair. His bottom lip quivering, he wrung his hands together in a gesture that was almost one of begging. He seemed in danger of bursting into tears. "You're Karl's—and my—only hope," he said in a defeated voice. "If you don't help us we're lost!"

Not daring to look him in the eye, I got to my feet and quietly trudged across the plush shag carpet. As I turned to close his apartment door behind me, I caught a final glimpse of Helmut, who had sunk into one of his expensive chairs. He was hunched over a piece of silver foil, pouring a white substance that looked like powder onto it. As I watched, transfixed, he noticed that I was still there.

"Get out, kid!" he yelled. I didn't need to be told twice.

I was beginning to regret ever meeting Karl Muller and getting involved in his shady business. I resolved once and for all to forget about the strange little man with the funny glasses. It wasn't that I didn't feel sorry for him. Something inside me didn't like the thought of his getting hurt, but I recognized that what was going on was way over my head. Way over *everyone's* head, for that matter. It was part of a sinister world that I had no wish to belong to. All I wanted was to go back to school and the mundane school yard skirmishes and boring classes. Head bowed, I marched toward the center of town as it began to rain.

"Come with us, sonny!"

Lost in my thoughts, I had been totally unaware of the two figures walking briskly behind me. Before I realized what was happening, I felt powerful hands on my shoulders. In desperation I tried to wriggle away from their steely grip.

"Struggling'll do you no good," said the same voice.

I turned to look at my two assailants, terrified that I was about to spend another couple of hours in the company of the Rhino and his friend. But the speaker wasn't either of the men who had kidnapped me at the end of the summer. It was somebody else. The trouble was, he looked equally unfriendly.

CHAPTER SEVEN

The puddles at my feet were covered in a thin layer of oil that reflected my glum face and the colorful carnival lights around me. In my right hand I clutched a large, pink cotton candy. From time to time I raised the sticky monstrosity to my lips, more out of habit than anything else. I didn't feel like eating. I felt sick. From a pair of gigantic loudspeakers someone was singing the words "Hello, I love you" in a voice that echoed through the rain. The voice mingled with the happy screams of children as they were spun through the air on an enormous metallic wheel of flashing lights.

I had no idea why my kidnappers had decided to bring me to a carnival. All I knew was that while my right hand was occupied with the cotton candy, my left was being gripped firmly by a short, fat man who called himself Horst. Well into his fifties, and with a thick, gray mustache, Horst had been squeezed beside me during the car ride here. He seemed to be continually sucking on a peppermint.

His companion and driver of the car went by the name of Max. He had been the one who insisted on buying me the horrible cotton candy. Max had the weatherbeaten face of a sailor. An immense set of bushy eyebrows hung over his deep set, suspicious eyes. He wore a wide-brimmed hat, giving him the appearance of a gangster. Despite this, I had to admit that neither man possessed quite the frightening menace of the Rhino.

"Make 'em young these days, don't they?" yelled Max above the din.

"Sure do," the other man affirmed.

We pushed our way slowly through the crowds. The ground had been turned to mud by the rain.

From either side came the harsh glare of cheap carnival game booths. To my dismay Max stopped at one and pulled me toward him. "Cheer up," he whispered in my ear. "It might never happen!"

I felt as if it already had! Once again I was the hostage of two complete strangers with unknown intentions. I silently cursed Karl Muller, the cause of all my problems.

"It's one mark for three shots," croaked a gruff female voice. "Hit the bullseye and you win a prize."

I looked on as Max handed a fistful of coins to the owner of the voice and pointed at me. As the woman reached across the wooden counter, wispy strands of mottled blond hair hung limply over her gaunt features. Opening her mouth to reveal a set of brown gravestone teeth, she carefully handed me three small lead pellets.

I glanced at my two companions and thought I'd better go along with the game. Besides, I'd done this before. On the counter were several air pistols attached to rusty chains. Taking one of the guns, I inserted a pellet into a small hole located at one end of the barrel and snapped it shut. Grudgingly, I took aim at a small target about 12 feet away from where I was standing and fired.

I scowled as Max, Horst, and the woman all began to laugh. I had missed. Stone-faced I repeated the exercise until all my pellets were gone.

"Hard luck, sonny," shrugged the woman. "Try again?"

As I shook my head in refusal, Max stepped forward and produced some more coins. "Let me have a try," he announced confidently.

Wrapping his left hand around the wrist of his right, with which he clutched the gun, Max assumed a combat position and took aim. I stole a look at the collection of gaudily colored plush animals that were the reward for those with greater accuracy than I. I felt a great empathy for them. After all, they were trapped in the same situation as I was— we were all unwilling prisoners patiently waiting for freedom.

Max also missed with all three shots.

"Blasted thing's been tampered with!" he shouted. "It veers to the left!"

He flung the gun down in disgust.

"Are you calling me a cheat?" snapped the woman.

"Let it go, Max," urged Horst, nudging his companion in the ribs.

With the woman's eyes following us, we retreated back into the crowd. I managed to get rid of the cotton candy as Horst and Max led me toward the line for the ghost train ride.

"Who are you?" I asked, finally getting up enough courage to speak as I wiped the pink, fluffy strands from my mouth.

"Hasn't your friend Helmut told you?" said Horst.

Before I had the chance to answer, Max interrupted. "You really a hacker, kid?" he asked. "You don't look old enough to shave."

"Helmut did tell us that he was recruiting young," the other man reminded him.

"Yeah, but I didn't take that to mean he'd be robbing the cradle!"

There was something about the two men that seemed strange. It didn't take me long to realize what it was. It was their voices: despite speaking perfect German both of my captors had the slightest tinge of an accent that betrayed the fact that they were strangers here.

"That's one mark apiece," said a new voice.

"C'mon, kid," smiled Max. "Let's have some fun!"

We had reached the front of the line and were being ushered into a small, red, round-nosed cart that had four wooden seats. Max climbed in first, and I wearily sat down beside him. Horst took the rear seat. There was a rumble as the cart began to move and suddenly we were plunged into darkness.

"So what's your specialty?" whispered Max as the cart began to pick up speed.

I had no idea what he was talking about and stared bleakly into the darkness.

"Hello! Anyone home? I said what's your specialty?"

"Huh?" I grunted, realizing that the man must have been talking to me.

This time he spoke more slowly. "What language do you specialize in? You *know*—computer hacking!"

"I hope he's better at computer piracy than he is at

speaking," said the sarcastic voice of Horst.

Suddenly I understood. The two men thought I was a hacker! They were asking me technical questions about computer programming.

Ahead of us, there was a sudden eruption of light and a skeletal figure appeared before us, its red eyes glowing and its empty mouth emitting a piercing banshee wail. Then, just as quickly, it went dark again.

"I'm sorry," I exclaimed, "you don't understand..."

Before I could finish my sentence, I was interrupted by Horst. "Listen to him," he sniggered. "Just because we'll never see 30 again he thinks we won't know what he's talking about."

As he finished speaking, the cart swerved left and we found ourselves looking at a giant spider's web. Perched at the center of the web was a huge luminous green spider. Behind me someone gasped.

As the cart moved on, Max spoke again. "You'd be surprised, sonny," he smiled. "We're not as stupid as we look!"

I felt a hot blast of peppermint-scented breath on the back of my neck. Horst had leaned over the back seat to place his head close to my own. He spoke in a quiet, serious voice, right into my ear: "Enough of this idle chatter. The reason we've picked you up is because we want you to give Helmut a message."

I shrugged.

"Tell Helmut that we're very happy with the material he gave us last week," Horst continued. "Tell him that his paymasters are also pleased."

Once more an eerie figure appeared in the darkness. A robed king walked slowly toward us holding his head under his arm. "I can seeeee youuuu!" he yowled.

Max waited for the apparition to disappear into the darkness before speaking again. "Tell Helmut also that we want more—much more," he said menacingly. "Time is running out and we need as much information as we can get."

"Tell him to strike at the U.S. bases," said the voice of Horst. "He'll be paid well for this information."

The barrage of instructions left me even more confused. "But *who* are you?" I asked.

There was silence for a few moments.

"Who do you think we are?" said Horst. "We're the people who pay your wages. We're the people who finance your operations. If you didn't already know it, you're now part of our team. You answer to us."

"And if you really didn't already know it, then Helmut isn't doing his job and deserves a severe reprimand!" the man sitting next to me added, his voice laden with menace.

Suddenly I understood. "You're from the KGB!" I proclaimed.

There was a jolt; then our cart began to climb, and I thought I felt something touching me in the darkness. The hairs on the back of my neck stood on end. A trickle of cold liquid was running down my face; some unseen monster had squirted water at us. For a few seconds, piercing screams from the others passengers in the ghost train filled the air.

"Watch what you're saying, kid," whispered Max, when the noise had died away. "Children should be seen and not heard!" There was the hint of a threat in his voice.

"Look son," interjected the other man quietly, "you've been recruited by Helmut to get information for the organization that we work for. Do the job well and you'll be equally well rewarded. Do the job badly and..." His voice trailed off as a beam of bright light appeared to signify that our ride was over. The carriage began to slow down.

"Why can't you give him the message yourself?" I asked.

"Good question," replied Horst. "Truth is we could if we wanted to—it's just that we sometimes like to personally interview any new additions to our happy little team. It's good business practice."

"And we like you, kid." Max's voice was patronizing now.

"Yes," agreed Horst, "it's obvious that you're in a different league from that freak in the sunglasses."

It was clear who they were talking about. "You mean Karl?" I asked.

"Yeah, that's him," replied Horst. "Looks like a weirdo but

apparently he's one of Helmut's best."

"Lousy taste in cars though," butted in Max.

As the cart drew to a halt I stepped from the seat as if in a trance. Things were getting more and more confusing. Did these men seriously believe that I, a 14-year-old schoolboy, had been drafted to join a team of hackers? And were they *really* from the KGB? If they were, then who were Rhino and his smiling friend? Could they be members of the FBI? I decided that now was not the time to ask these questions. And I reminded myself that I would never again have anything to do with Karl Muller. In the future, at the very mention of his name I was going to retire to my bedroom and bury my head under the safety of my blankets.

"That wasn't such a big deal," declared Horst as we rejoined the crowds and moved away from the ghost train.

"Waste of money," agreed his friend, winking at me. "Next time we'll find a more conventional place to hold our little *tête-a-têtes*."

Much to my relief we slowly headed toward the exit of the fairground, and Max indicated that I was free to go. But as I scurried toward the leafy streets of Hanover, the voice of Horst called me back.

Holding a package of peppermints in his outstretched hand he gave me a look that was colder than the fall breeze. "We'll be seeing you again, no doubt," he said. "And we'll be looking forward to seeing the fruits of your labors."

Max leaned out of the car window. "And don't forget to give that message to Helmut," he said.

CHAPTER EIGHT

I never did give the message to Helmut. Somehow I hoped that by staying away from the whole mess it would just go away. Of course, things are never quite that simple. Fate seemed to have decided that Karl Muller and I would meet again.

In the meantime, I tried my best to settle back into normality. I tried to go back to being the boy I had been before the whole thing had started. School, homework, parents, and teachers became the dominant forces of my life. But things had changed. All too often, I would find myself distracted by thoughts of Karl and Helmut. In class, I would frequently be caught daydreaming by irate teachers. I couldn't help it. Despite everything, I still wanted to know what had happened to that strange pair of computer hackers.

From my schoolboy point of view, the whole of Germany seemed to be in some kind of low during the winter of 1986. In a funny sort of way it had seemed to start when the West German soccer team lost to Argentina in the World Cup Final at the end of the summer. After that a strange mood of lethargy seemed to settle over everything. Now we were in the grip of a severe winter, the kind that has to be seen to be believed. The snow is capable of laying siege to Germany with an almost military precision. Within days of its arrival, movement around the cities can be rendered practically impossible.

Perhaps my grim recollections of that time are slightly affected by the deep depression I found myself in. There are some people today who blame the strange, confused state I was in that winter on an addiction. An addiction to danger. A yearning to go back to the perilous world of espionage that I had tried so hard to break away from. Whatever the reason, my thoughts were more concerned with Karl than with Christmas. I felt as if I'd gotten almost to the end of a really exciting book—and then had to put it away without finishing the story.

Then one day in early December I received a letter that promised to put an end to my torment. It was from Karl. Like Helmut's before him, Karl's letter was brief and to the point. It read: Come and see me on Saturday. Be careful not to be seen—KM.

Although in my heart I knew that nothing but trouble could come from agreeing to the meeting, I knew right away that I had to go. No matter what the consequences, the questions inside my head had to be answered. So it was with some trepidation that a few days later I found myself walking up to the doorway of Karl Muller's apartment. I'd taken the advice of the letter and wrapped myself in a bulky overcoat; to be on the safe side I'd worn a scarf and hat as well. If the Rhino or any of his chums were lying in wait for me, I wanted to be sure that I was as anonymous as possible.

Karl could hardly hide his pleasure at seeing me. "You look older," he said.

His apartment was even more filthy than I remembered it. I was surprised to see that now, even the computer was home to a coating of dust and cigarette ash. That was a bad sign—Karl must be in real trouble if he couldn't even be bothered to clean his beloved computer.

The computer, however, was at least up and running, and its screen was currently filled with a foreign language. "Nothing ever changes," Karl smiled grimly, gesturing toward it. This time he was not wearing his sunglasses.

Out of habit, I looked at his T-shirt to see what new cryptic message was displayed there, but there was none. He was dressed in funereal black. With a shrug I removed my coat, and a shower of powdery snow fell onto the shabby carpet. "Careful!" said Karl in mock outrage. "Don't mess the place up!"

"I got your letter," I said.

"Yes, I wanted to see you. I've been informed that you've had some more visitors."

"Is that *why* you wanted to see me?" I asked.

"Sort of. But there's something else as well."

"Oh?"

"I like you, kid," he said softly. His shoulders bowed, and he gazed at me mournfully. "And the truth is, I haven't seen anybody since the last time you were here."

"You've been alone since then?" I gasped. It was hard to believe.

"The net is closing in," he said with fear in his eyes. "It's not a game anymore. Those people who picked you up the last time I saw you were probably from the CIA or the FBI, not the KGB as I'd assumed."

"I thought so," I confirmed dryly.

For the next couple of hours as we worked our way through cup after cup of coffee, Karl Muller finally told me the full story. I don't know why he chose to do so. I got a weird feeling that somehow he thought that by telling me his tale he could unload his guilt. Either that or he instinctively knew that this might be his last opportunity to impress somebody. As he spoke, his mood seemed to swing between pride and despair.

"It all started about two years ago when I met Helmut," he explained. "At the time I was working as a computer programmer. I never in a million years thought it would come to this."

He opened a fresh pack of cigarettes and raised one to his trembling lips. "Helmut said that he knew of a quick way of making money. Lots of it. He told me he was looking for a specialist in UNIX. It is a computer language that I know a lot about."

Karl blew out a stream of smoke and continued.

"At first it was easy. All I had to do was get onto the Internet and gain access to electronic mail by guessing passwords."

"How did you do that?" I asked.

"It's not difficult," Karl explained. "Computer security is practically nonexistent. Most of the time I would just enter the name "GUEST" and find that the password was usually

45

the same. People are so stupid.

"Once into a system I would ferret around; read electronic mail and gain access to other bases. Eventually I was able to get into top secret bases around the world. It was easy money. I couldn't believe how easy. Soon I was able to give up my job, buy expensive cars, and devote all of my time to hacking."

"But where does the KGB come into all this?" I inquired.

"I didn't know it was the KGB at first," said Karl. "I wasn't supposed to know that the money Helmut was giving me was coming directly from the Russians. When I finally found out, I told him that I wanted to stop. He warned me that I'd find myself in serious trouble if I did." I looked at Karl's hands and noticed that they were shaking as he spoke.

"Helmut is bad news," Karl continued. "He's a very dangerous guy. He needs the information that I can give him to keep the KGB happy. He likes the high life and uses the money to pay for—well, let's just say he's picked up some unhealthy habits."

"What do you mean?" I asked as his voice trailed off.

"Helmut likes to indulge in things you'd be better off not knowing about," Karl went on. "It was only later that I realized that he had been using me to pay for those—er—shall we say *seedier* parts of his life."

I thought of Helmut hunched over his silver foil, pouring out the white powder.

Karl took a final drag on his cigarette and then stubbed it out, scowling.

"It was when I discovered those SDINET files that things started to go wrong," he said bitterly.

"You mean that gold mine you discovered?" I said, remembering his excitement.

"Gold mine!" Karl snorted. "It turned out to be fool's gold. Those files had been planted by someone in the West to trap me. They were just the bait, and I fell for it hook, line, and sinker. Stupid!" He smacked himself on the forehead with the heel of his hand.

"I don't understand," I said.

"It was only when the KGB did some research into SDINET that they realized we'd been tricked. SDINET was a sort of Trojan horse—false documents that had been planted to sound important so that my phone could be traced while I was wasting hours downloading them into my computer."

I shook my head. "That's devious."

"Very devious," agreed my frightened friend. "So devious that it worked. So devious that it left the KGB very angry with Helmut for being careless enough to give them the files. And that left Helmut extremely angry with me. I should have been more careful—after all, I've been doing this for almost two years!"

Like a condemned man, Karl dug into the pack of cigarettes that lay beside his chair and clumsily lit one. "So now I'm a virtual prisoner in my own apartment," he trembled. "Whenever I leave the place, I can feel eyes watching me. I know it's only a matter of time before they move in for me."

"What will happen if they catch you?" I asked.

"Don't know," he shrugged. "I could be tried for spying; it will almost certainly mean prison. *Anything* could happen!"

There was silence for a few moments as my friend's gaze wandered over the contents of his apartment—the piles of garbage on the threadbare carpet, the overflowing ashtrays, the towering heaps of yellowing computer printouts. I could imagine his thoughts as he reflected on the trouble Helmut's so-called easy money had brought to him.

"All I ever wanted to do was use my computer," he muttered at last. "I didn't mean to become a criminal—it just seemed like a big adventure!" He sighed. "If only I could go back in time..."

There was another long silence as we both reflected on the hopelessness of Karl's situation. I was still searching my brain for something encouraging to say when he suddenly seemed to pull himself together a little. Hoisting his thin frame from the easy chair, he grasped my hand. "You'd better go now," he said, smiling weakly. "I shouldn't have

47

asked you here. I got myself into this mess, it's up to me to get myself out of it."

We walked in silence to the front door of his apartment. Karl made me stand in the shadows while he checked to see if anyone was hanging around outside. When he was satisfied that the coast was clear, he gestured for me to leave. "Go quickly," he urged. "Don't come back."

The snow had transformed the streets into a picture postcard as I made my way home. This time I really did think the story of Karl Muller had finally come to an end. I felt a strange mixture of relief and regret.

CHAPTER NINE

But still Karl Muller refused to go away. Even though our last meeting had more or less cleared up every question that had been nagging away at my brain, I found it impossible to return to everyday life. The computer hacker and I seemed to be somehow linked by fate. Try as I might, I couldn't exorcise him from my life.

A week had passed since my visit to Karl's squalid apartment. In that week I had made every possible effort to get back into some kind of normal routine. The fact that school vacation had arrived was a big help. No more school! I was determined to put all my energy into the serious task of enjoying myself.

For a while I succeeded. I started to see more of my old friends. We would spend our days playing in the snow, tobogganing, and taking part in snowball fights—just being normal, rowdy kids. For the first time in months I felt relaxed and at peace; the burden of Karl Muller seemed to have finally slipped from my shoulders. I began to regain the carefree attitude that I had had before I'd been unwittingly dragged into the world of computer hacking.

But it didn't last. One crisp day in January, I was playing with my friends in a park about a mile and a half from my home. The snow had fallen particularly thickly the previous night, and the screams and yelps of the children were sharp and clear in the winter air. A glorious yellow Sun that wouldn't have been out of place in the height of summer was shining, its glittering rays making the blanket of snow look like polished marble.

The afternoon was drawing to a close when I suddenly became aware that there was something happening on the west side of the park. The first thing I noticed was a subtle change in the tone of the children's screams. They weren't play-screams anymore. They were screams of genuine fear.

Looking into the distance through the park railings I saw the reason for this transformation. In the middle of the idyllic winter scene was a stream of black smoke billowing slowly into the skies. There was a fire. And whatever it was that was burning was already surrounded by a group of morbid sightseers.

I joined the crowd of spectators steadily moving toward the scene. It soon became evident that the fire didn't emanate from a house or any other kind of building. It seemed to be coming from something else. Something smaller. It was not until I was standing 100 feet away from the scene that I saw what was burning. Someone had a set a car on fire.

A horde of around 50 people had gathered to observe the flaming spectacle. In the distance I heard the sound of approaching fire engines. Wanting a closer look, I squeezed and pushed my way through the crowd of gaping onlookers until I was right at the front, and the heat of the flaming vehicle was on my face. And then I gave a gasp of shock.

I had seen this car before. Its once-sleek exterior was veiled by a cloud of thick, black smoke belching from the melting engine, and its red paint work was blistered and bubbled. But there was no mistaking it. It was Karl Muller's sports car.

As if that were not enough, there was another shock to come.

"Poor devil," said someone in the crowd. "He can't have known what hit him!"

Until that moment, I hadn't noticed that the driver was still inside the car. Now I saw his still-burning body, engulfed by orange and yellow flames, slumped behind the steering wheel. With a shout of dismay I broke out from the crowd and skidded through the snow toward the car to get a closer look, but an onlooker caught me and held me back. An overwhelming smell of burning gasoline filled the air. I craned my neck as I peered through the smoke, desperately looking for some clue to the driver's identity.

He was wearing the charred remnants of a sheepskin coat.

I sifted through my memory, trying to recall where I had seen that coat before. Then I remembered. I remembered that day in The Friendly Café when Karl's friend Helmut had come in hugging a sheepskin coat to his body. It was the *same* coat. That meant only one thing—it was Helmut sitting inside the burning car.

Coughing and reeling, I forced my way back through the tight circle of onlookers. As a pair of fire engines arrived on the scene and began dousing the burned-out shell of the car with their hoses, I ran toward the exit of the park.

The snow began to fall thickly again, and my mind whirled with images of spies, KGB, FBI, the burning body of Helmut, and the mocking face of the Rhino. My heart pounded. I didn't care who was watching as I raced toward Karl's apartment, stumbling and sliding through the snow. I *had* to tell Karl. I had to warn him that he might be in trouble.

CHAPTER TEN

"Let me in!" I yelled, bunching my freezing fingers into fists and hammering as hard as I could on the peeling paint of Karl's front door. "It's me! Let me in!"

After what seemed an eternity, there was a creaking noise, and the door opened a crack to reveal a pair of fearful eyes staring out at me. "Go away," hissed the voice of Karl Muller.

"Let me in!" I repeated urgently through a haze of frosty breath. "Open the door!"

Karl reluctantly obeyed. He slammed the door shut as soon as I had entered.

"I've told you not to come here!" he said brusquely.

For what was to be the last time, I made my way into Karl's living room. As I paused to catch my breath, I was surprised to see that he appeared to have been making some attempt to tidy up the place. Then I realized that he was in the middle of packing. The table that was usually home to his beloved computer now stood bare. Only a dusty outline where Karl's pride and joy had once stood remained to remind us of the instrument at the heart of all our troubles. Around the room were boxes and cartons filled to the brim with Karl's belongings. Floppy disks and computer printouts were strewn around the frayed carpet like confetti.

"Leaving?" I asked, already knowing the answer to my question.

He nodded. "You shouldn't have come. You've got to leave immediately!" His voice was brimming over with despair.

"I've come to warn you," I replied. "I've just seen your car!"

The blood drained from Karl's face.

"Helmut borrowed it. He's supposed to have brought it back this morning."

"You're not going to get it back now," I said. "When I saw it an hour ago it was on fire!"

Now the color returned to Karl's face as quickly as it had

disappeared. It went from pure white to the brightest crimson.

"My car!" he yelled. "Please tell me you're kidding!"

"I'm not joking!" I shouted back. "It was on fire, and I think Helmut was still sitting in it."

For a moment I thought that Karl was going to collapse. Unable to speak, he sank to his knees, and holding his head in his hands, began to rock backward and forward. From the back of his throat came an awful gurgling noise, like the sound of a drowning man. I noticed that printed on his white T-shirt in big black letters were the words: People are strange.

"Get up, Karl, get up!" I urged.

But it was already too late. As the words left my lips there was a thunderous banging on the front door that made the whole apartment shake. And then there were voices. "Open up!" they shouted. "It's the police."

Like an ostrich burying its head in the sand, Karl wrapped his childish hands around his head and groaned. It seemed as if he'd finally given up.

Trying to fight back the rising panic, I glanced around desperately for a means of escape. Any second now the apartment was going to be invaded by the police. Helmut was dead, Karl was about to be arrested for computer piracy, and there was no telling *what* was going to happen to me. If the KGB could be tricked into believing that I was a hacker, what would our own police think?

The police were obviously not going to wait any longer for someone to answer the door. Three more sharp bangs on the door were followed by a deafening sound of splintering wood —then, amid a confusion of shouts and stamping feet, two familiar figures stormed into the room.

Brandishing a pair of shining silver handcuffs, the first figure rushed straight to the quivering Karl, hauled him up by the scruff of the neck and, in a businesslike voice, began to read him his rights. Through my fear, I recognized the man instantly. He was the one who had driven the car to that deserted warehouse earlier that year. If he had reminded me of a demon then, his current appearance certainly did nothing to change that opinion.

After a moment, however, my attention focused on the second person to enter the room. Carrying another set of handcuffs and heading straight toward me, was the Rhino.

Dwarfed by his massive bulk, I raised my eyes to meet his. For a frozen moment, he didn't speak, but stared coldly back at me, slowly shaking his bulbous head. Then, as my knees knocked together and my teeth chattered, he raised one of his gigantic hands and gently pushed me in the chest. The force of the push sent me flying backward, and I landed on Karl's sofa, sending a pile of computer disks spinning through the air.

Rhino gazed down with contempt at my sprawling body. "Some people never learn," he muttered. In the background, I could hear Karl whimpering with fear.

Rhino heard it, too. He wheeled around and strode purposefully over to where my friend was cowering, handcuffed and trembling. "We've been watching you for almost a year, you know," he said nonchalantly. "You didn't really think you could get away with it, did you?"

By now several more people had entered the room. Dressed in standard police uniforms, they began to sort briskly through the boxes of computer equipment that Karl had been hastily packing away.

"Planning a vacation, were you?" sneered the Rhino, scornfully surveying the collection of hurriedly packed cardboard boxes. "Don't worry, we'll find you somewhere nice and comfortable to stay!"

"Better keep it official," his comrade reminded him. "We don't want any mistakes."

The Rhino gave a nod of his head and reached into the inside pocket of his coat. From where I was sitting I could just make out the letters "FBI" that were embossed on the shiny badge that he waved in Karl's direction.

I breathed hard. So my suspicions had been correct! The lumbering Rhino and his smiling friend *were* agents of the FBI. Now their attentions returned to me.

"What about the boy?" said the Rhino's companion.

"What about him?" replied the Rhino. "He's an accessory. He's known about this all along. He'll be going to the same place as his friend."

My stomach lurched. Once again I was sincerely regretting ever meeting Karl Muller. I stared over at the computer hacker, whose head was hanging low. I could see a tear running down his nose.

I blinked, trying to resign myself to my fate. When I looked up, the Rhino and his friend were whispering to one another, and for an instant I was reminded of being back in the warehouse with them.

Suddenly the first man spoke again, but this time there was no trace of a false smile on his face. "Get up and go," he said calmly. "We know that you've got nothing to do with this mess. Anyway, you're too young to be convicted."

"You're a lucky young man," growled the Rhino. There was a hint of disappointment in his voice.

The other man beckoned me closer. "Before you go," he said quietly, "let me give you a little advice: Don't play with things you don't understand. If you do you'll get your fingers burned."

The image of Helmut in the flaming car flashed before me.

"And let me give you something as well!" The sound of the Rhino's voice was followed by a tremendous blow from his open hand. It caught my left ear, sending a bolt of electricity down my spine and momentarily deafening me.

"Now go!" he yelled.

I didn't need telling twice. Jumping to my feet I was out of the room in seconds. The laughing voices of the Rhino and his accomplice echoed behind me as I bolted like a frightened deer. I didn't pause to look behind me. I didn't even bother to pick up my coat.

CHAPTER ELEVEN

Of course, all of this happened ten years ago, but the memory of Karl Muller and the sinister web of intrigue that I found myself drawn into still refuses to fade. To this day I am haunted by nightmares filled with images of the Rhino and the charred body of Helmut. Yet I feel that the experience has taught me a valuable lesson: Don't tamper with things you don't understand.

As I head toward my mid-twenties I often pause to reflect on what might have happened had I not encountered Karl Muller. Or rather, what might *not* have happened. When I sit behind my own computer and look back on the events of years ago, it's difficult not to feel a strange sense of gratitude toward Karl. After all, if we hadn't met I would never have developed an interest in computer technology. I would never have possessed the confidence to start my own software company. And I certainly wouldn't have had the diligence to be always on the lookout for impostors on my own computer network. They're out there, you know.

Nowadays, to represent a threat to your property a burglar doesn't have to come from the same part of town. Or the same city. Or, for that matter, the same country. Because as the Internet has encouraged the free movement of information throughout every part of the globe, so it has extended the boundaries of those who make a living by stealing the possessions of others. And believe me, they get more and more devious with each passing year.

Whenever I tell people my story, I'm often tempted to adjust the ending slightly in order to paint a less cowardly picture of myself. I suppose there's no shame in wanting to be seen as brave and worthy rather than weak and frightened. Yet somehow, on reaching the climax of my tale I can never quite find it in myself to lie. When I'm asked what I did when the Rhino struck me with the giant palm of his hand, there's only one thing I can say.

I ran, I tell them. I ran.

GLOSSARY

APPLICATION
A program that enables the user to create, enter, and design information. Examples are word processors, spreadsheets, and paint programs.

ASCII
(AMERICAN STANDARD CODE FOR INFORMATION INTERCHANGE)
A standard computer text format in which each character is represented by seven bits.

BBS
(BULLETIN BOARD SYSTEM)
A telecommunications facility used to share information with others through the use of a modem and specialized software.

BASIC
(BEGINNER'S ALL-PURPOSE SYMBOLIC INSTRUCTION CODE)
A common programming language that is easy to learn.

BINARY
A numbering system based on a series of ones (1s) and zeros (0s). The binary code uses the ones and zeros to represent information.

BIT
(BINARY DIGIT)
The smallest possible unit of computer information —either the digit one (1) or zero (0).

BOMB
The abnormal termination of a program. A bomb occurs when a program unexpectedly halts because of a bug, or when a program encounters data conditions it cannot handle.

BOOT
To start up a computer by loading its operating system into memory.

BUG
A problem in a software program that was originally named after a moth that caused the failure of an early computer in 1945 at Harvard University. Nowadays, the term "bug" generally refers to an inaccurate line of programming code that causes the software to bomb or execute incorrectly.

BYTE
A collection of bits that make up a single piece of information that is equivalent to one character of the alphabet. A byte is made up of eight bits; it has eight ones and zeros per byte.

CIA
(CENTRAL INTELLIGENCE AGENCY)
U.S. agency set up in the late 1940s to protect the government from hostile foreign nations. The CIA employs agents in over 150 countries to send back information, which it then assesses, offering its analysis to other U.S. agencies. The CIA also attempts to prevent any risk to national security posed by foreign spies.

CPU
(CENTRAL PROCESSING UNIT)
The computer's main information processor, usually a single silicon chip called a microprocessor.

CRASH
Another term for when a computer bombs.

DATA
Also called information. This is processed by the computer.

DATABASE
A collection of related information organized for storage and retrieval. This may contain, for example, telephone numbers and addresses.

DIRECTORY
An onscreen listing of the contents of a computer.

DISK DRIVE
A disk drive holds disks that can retrieve and store information from the computer. There are two kinds of disk drives. A floppy disk (3.5 inch) drive holds the floppy disk that the user inserts into the computer. A hard disk drive contains a built-in disk that is permanently installed.

DISK SERVER
A disk drive, usually on a network, that is available to all users.

DOCUMENT
Information stored on a disk.

DOS
(DISK OPERATING SYSTEM)
The name of an operating system. Every computer needs this type of software in order to function.

DOWNLOAD
A procedure in which a user transfers data from a computer's database to their own computer and stores the data on either a hard or floppy disk.

E-MAIL
(ELECTRONIC MAIL)
A messaging system that enables the user to send and receive "mail" to and from other people on the electronic network. A message can be as simple or as complex as required.

ENCRYPTION
Similar to coding, the substitution of characters to hide the contents of a document.

ETHERNET
A means of transferring large amounts of data between computers via network cables.

FAX
(FACSIMILE TRANSMISSION)
The transmission of printed pages through a telecommunications device such as a telephone.

FBI
(FEDERAL BUREAU OF INVESTIGATION)
Division of the U.S. Justice Department, run from the national headquarters in Washington, D.C. The FBI is the most important investigating division of the government. Part of the Bureau deals with law enforcement and looks into federal crimes, including kidnapping, espionage, and treason. The FBI also gathers information on people or groups that could threaten national security.

FILE
Information stored on a disk. Also called a document.

FLOPPY DISK
A 3.5-inch flexible disk held in a rigid plastic casing. It is inserted into the floppy disk drive of a computer.

FREEWARE
Software that doesn't cost the user anything. It is produced with the intention that it will be distributed throughout a large number of users.

GNU-EMACS
A computer program used in e-mailing. This was discovered to contain a bug that enabled users to gain access to a computer's system files.

HARD DRIVE
A permanently installed disk that is capable of holding vast quantities of information. The hard drive may be inside or outside a computer.

HARDWARE
The physical parts of the computer. The screen, keyboard, mouse, disk drives, casing, and all the electronic mechanisms and boards held inside the computer.

INTERNET
An electronic network linking computers all over the world.

KGB
A government agency of the former Soviet Union. The letters "KGB" are an abbreviation of the words "Committee for State Security" in Russian. Its main function was to ensure that the Communist Party kept control of the Soviet Union. It operated a secret police force and was also involved with gathering information about other countries and secretly aiding foreign governments or other organizations that it considered sympathetic to the Soviet Union. The KGB was disbanded in 1991 when the Soviet Union was dissolved.

MAINFRAME
A large computer shared by many users.

MEGABYTE (M)
A measure of size representing 1,048,576 bytes of storage capacity on a disk or in RAM.

MICROCOMPUTER
A small and inexpensive computer designed for home use.

MICROPROCESSOR
A minute silicon chip containing a huge number of electronic components.

MODEM (MODULATOR/DEMODULATOR)
A device that allows computers to communicate via telephone lines.

MONITOR
A computer screen.

MOUSE
A hand-held device used to navigate across a computer screen.

PERSONAL COMPUTER (PC)
A computer designed to be used in the home or small business setting.

PROGRAM
A set of instructions, usually in the form of a programming language, that tells the computer what to do.

COMPUTER LANGUAGE
A language used to write programs for a computer. There are many languages, including C++, BASIC, FORTRAN, and SmallTalk/V.

PROTOCOL

A set of rules and procedures that determines how information travels between computers.

PUBLIC DOMAIN SOFTWARE

Software that can be copied without infringement of copyright.

RAM
(RANDOM-ACCESS MEMORY)

The part of the computer's memory that allows for temporary storage of information. Because RAM is only temporary, any information left in RAM is lost when the computer is turned off.

ROM
(READ-ONLY MEMORY)

The part of a computer's memory that permanently stores information.

REBOOT

To restart the computer.

SHAREWARE

Copyrighted computer programs that can be used on a trial basis.

SOFTWARE

Computer programs used to instruct the computer hardware how to perform certain tasks.

SYSTEM FILE

A file that contains information that the computer uses to operate and start up.

SYSTEM SOFTWARE

The software required by the computer to run correctly.

TELECOMMUNICATIONS

Sharing information over phone lines through the

use of a modem.

UNIX
An operating system developed by Bell Laboratories for computers. UNIX permits the simultaneous running of several programs at once and is regarded as a powerful general-purpose operating system.

UPLOAD
A procedure in which a user transfers information from their own computer to a remote computer.

USER GROUP
A group of people who have an interest in a particular computer or particular computer program.

VIRUS
A computer program that is designed to alter the normal functioning of a computer by destroying data, corrupting system files, or locking users out of the system. In many cases, the user may be unaware that a virus exists in the system until it is too late to protect the existing data. A virus is generally passed from disk to disk, or through telecommunications file transfer.

WORLDWIDE WEB
Another name for the Internet.

BIOGRAPHIES

The story contains fictional characters investigating
a true-life mystery. Before you look at the facts and
make up your own mind, here's a brief biography of
the characters:

HELMUT
(ACTUAL CHARACTER—DISGUISED NAME)

A computer hacker involved with Internet crime
to finance his drug habit. Helmut worked for the
KGB, who provided him with his list of targets. He
felt that he could make more money if he got
assistance from hackers who were more skilled
than he was. Loosely based on real-life hacker
Karl Koch.

MAX AND HORST (FICTIONAL)

KGB agents acting as a point of contact between
the hackers and their paymasters. Responsible for
keeping the individual members of the group
under surveillance.

KARL MULLER
(ACTUAL CHARACTER—DISGUISED NAME)

The computer hacker who found a way of using
the Internet to tap into top secret bases in the
United States and worldwide in order to steal
information for the KGB. Loosely based on real-
life hacker Marcus Hess, he was arrested for
spying after falling into a trap set up by a U.S.
laboratory.

THE NARRATOR
(FICTIONAL)

A schoolboy from Hanover, Germany, unwittingly involved with a group of computer hackers working for the KGB after agreeing to run errands in return for money.

THE RHINO AND ACCOMPLICE
(FICTIONAL)

FBI agents investigating the group of computer hackers in order to obtain enough evidence to arrest Helmut's team.

CLASSIFIED FILES

How did the whole thing start? How could it be possible for a German hacker with a home computer to find his way into top secret U.S. files? What was he looking for? Who was responsible for the mysterious death of one of the team? And what role do the KGB and the FBI play in the story? Here are the answers to some of these questions:

HOW DID THE INTERNET INCIDENT START?

In the mid-eighties, computer hacking was already quite common—common enough for many hacking groups to have been established. One of the most famous in Germany was called the Chaos Club. It had nothing to do with spying; its purpose was merely to cause mischief by invading other people's computer systems. But it was at the Chaos Club that the spy ring at the center of the Internet Incident had its origin.

Karl Koch was a university dropout. He had a small inheritance but was quickly wasting it on drugs and high living. He needed a way to make lots of money, fast. His opportunity came when he had a chance meeting with an older man named Peter Kahl. Kahl was trying to set up a group of hackers capable of breaking into top secret military bases in the West, with the purpose of selling the information to the KGB. Koch decided to join the gang.

The Soviets gave him a long list of programs, information, passwords, and sites to hack into. But he knew his skills at hacking were not particularly brilliant, so he attended Chaos Club meetings to try to pick up valuable information on computer systems. It was there that he met a man whose skills were brilliant. He was Hans Huber, a 17-year-old expert in the VAX computer operating system. He was nicknamed "Pengo" after a penguin character in a popular computer game. At the time, Pengo, who also had drug problems, was unemployed and in need of money. He agreed to help.

There were now three in the gang: Kahl, Koch, and Pengo. But soon they needed an expert on UNIX systems. They turned to another member of the Chaos Club, Marcus Hess, who worked as a UNIX specialist. He was not involved with drugs, but he did have a passion for fast cars, which meant he needed lots of money. He, too, agreed to help.

Hess was a big success. Shortly after joining the other two hackers, he managed to download a copy of the UNIX source code for the KGB. They were delighted and paid the group's leader, Peter Kahl, 25,000 deutsche marks—the largest sum he had yet received from them.

By 1987, Hess had wormed his way into top-secret bases all over the United States and worldwide. But Koch and Pengo were becoming increasingly frightened by the whole business. After one of Koch's acquaintances from the Chaos Club was arrested for hacking, they decided to turn themselves in to the authorities. They asked for amnesty and, in turn, offered to provide information that would enable the net to close in on the many groups of German hackers that were operating all over the country.

On March 2, 1989, 18 hackers were arrested in a series of raids. They included Hess, Koch, Kahl, and Pengo. After a few days they were all released until the time of their trials. Two months later, however, the body of Karl Koch was discovered in some woods on the outskirts of Hanover. He had been burned to death. Had he lived, he would probably have shared the same fate as Pengo, who escaped trial because of the amnesty and went on to live a normal life.

Hess was not quite so lucky. He conducted his own defense but was found guilty of spying and was given a two-year prison sentence. After his release, he went back to the world of computers—this time legally. He became a computer software writer.

HOW DID THEY GET AWAY WITH IT?

The hackers would have been able to get away with it for even longer if it were not for the efforts of one man—Berkeley Laboratories' system administration manager, Clifford Stoll.

Here are some of the reasons why Hess, the hacker who found his way into Berkeley's system, was at first successful—and some of the reasons why he was eventually caught:

Hess was successful because:

Security was lax. Back in the 1980s, nobody had yet considered the possibility that the Internet might be used for serious crime. Quite often, all a hacker had to do to gain access to a company's e-mail was dial into their system and type in the user name "GUEST" and the password "GUEST." This is how Hess gained access to the private e-mail of Berkeley Laboratories. He was already an expert on UNIX, the computer system used by Berkeley that allowed the distribution of their e-mail. By reading this e-mail, he was able to enter other computer systems because of the carelessness of users. Messages such as **Gone on vacation—my UNIX password is "Taurus" if you need it** allowed the hacker to spread his net. Soon, using such plundered passwords, he was accessing other e-mail sites around the world.

He was provided with his targets. The KGB were the paymasters of the whole hacking group and gave them their list of targets—which included research laboratories, NASA's Jet Propulsion Laboratory, and even the Pentagon.

There was a bug in the system. It should have been impossible for the hacker, even after getting into the computer system, to wield any real power. But there was a fatal flaw in the e-mail system that Berkeley Laboratories was using—"Gnu-Emacs." This bug enabled the hacker to adjust his system privileges easily. Instead of being merely a guest user, he could take control of the whole system and cause havoc.

The hacker was clever. To enable him to work even more quickly and efficiently, he planted a program of his own in the Berkeley Laboratories system. The purpose of this program was to keep a record of all other user passwords in the system. Every time anyone logged on to Berkeley and typed in his or her password, it was duly recorded by the program to be used at a later date by the hacker.

He took precautions to avoid detection. The hacker was using a technique known as "network weaving," which involved diverting calls all around the United States. This was intended to disguise the fact that he was calling from outside the United States.

The hacker was caught because:

He made one small mistake. The hacker's presence on the computer system of Berkeley Laboratories had resulted in a slight error in the company's accounts. It was only 75 cents, but it was enough to attract the attention of Clifford Stoll. It was unfortunate for the hacker that Stoll decided to investigate—such an error is not unusual in the world of computers. Often it is caused by a small fault, or bug, in the programming code that tells the computer to carry out a certain action. (A recent example of such a bug was contained in Intel's Pentium chip, which, after a publicity campaign that made it a bestseller, was found to have a slight flaw that affected its ability to add figures.) But whereas most people would have been tempted to put the 75-cent shortfall down to experience, Clifford Stoll decided to investigate and so discovered that there was a hacker in the system.

The hacker was monitored. Wary of being detected as he watched the hacker's progress, Stoll rigged up an ingenious tripwire system. Every time the hacker entered Berkeley Laboratories' computers, Stoll was paged by his computer, and the hacker's exploits were documented on computer printouts that recorded the interloper's every keystroke. In this way Stoll began to maintain a 24-hour watch on the person who was becoming his opponent in what amounted to a digital chess match.

The hacker left clues. With a little more detective work, Clifford Stoll noticed that the majority of the hacker's passwords were of German derivation. He even began to gain an understanding of some of the hacker's personal habits. For example, from the passwords that the anonymous hacker used, Stoll was able to conclude that he smoked Benson and Hedges cigarettes.

The FBI got involved. Although they showed little interest when Berkeley first reported that they had a hacker on the system, the FBI joined in the hunt immediately after it became clear that the hacker was based outside the United States and that international espionage was involved. Because the files are still classified, we do not know exactly *what* part the FBI played, but certainly they were instrumental in tracking down the hackers.

The hacker fell for a trap set by Berkeley. Once he had been detected, the only thing preventing his capture was that he was never on the telephone long enough for an international trace to be completed. But Stoll proved to be as cunning as the anonymous person he was hunting. The young system manager planted a number of fake documents relating to a supposedly top secret project, which he named SDINET. Sure enough, the hacker took the bait and, because of the enormous amounts of fake SDINET data that Stoll had posted on his computers, the mysterious hacker spent hours on the telephone downloading the material. The trap was sprung, and the hacker was caught.

WHO KILLED KARL KOCH?

One of the most sinister aspects of the Internet Incident is that it resulted in the death of one of the hackers.

Two months after being released from custody pending trial, the body of Karl Koch was found in some woods on the outskirts of Hanover. He had last been seen on May 23, 1989, when he had turned up for work as usual at the Christian Democratic Party offices. At noon he had driven off alone to deliver a package across town. It was nine days before he was seen again. His body was eventually discovered near an abandoned car that was covered in filth and thick dust. His charred torso was lying next to an empty gasoline can; Koch had been burned to death. His death was given as suicide. But was it?

SUICIDE?

Karl Koch was a drug addict. One of the reasons he had gotten involved with the Internet spy ring was to pay for his habit. Now that the game was up, there was no way for him to make the vast amounts of money he needed. Maybe he decided that he couldn't go on without his drugs.

BUT:

Koch was actually getting treatment for his addiction at the time of his death. And he finally had a steady job, with the Christian Democratic Party. So it looks as if he was getting some kind of stability into his life at last. Why should he choose this time, just when things were looking brighter, to commit suicide?

Koch had been frightened enough by what he had gotten involved in to give himself up to the authorities. Maybe he was terrified of what might happen to him when the wheels of justice ground into action. Maybe the thought of serving a prison sentence was too much for him to bear.

BUT:

There was little chance of Koch's being prosecuted. He had traded information with the authorities in return for amnesty. If he had lived, there was every chance that he would have gone free—like his friend Pengo.

Koch was frightened of the KGB. They would have known that it was he who had informed the authorities about the computer hacking. Perhaps he felt they would pursue him until they had had their revenge and decided he would rather take things into his own hands.

BUT:

There was no evidence that the KGB was interested in taking revenge on anyone. All the other members of the group lived to tell the tale.

MURDER?

Koch's body was found lying near a gasoline can. But only the vegetation immediately around the the body was scorched and burned—it looked as if the fire had been controlled. If he had set fire to himself, surely the fire would have spread to a larger area? There had been no rain in that area for weeks.

The body was *barefoot*. Why would Koch have driven into the forest wearing no shoes? Was it more likely that he had been killed somewhere else, then taken into the woods and his body set on fire?

The police did investigate the death. When Germany was reunified in 1990, they asked for information about the incident. One rumor that resulted from these investigations was that Karl was murdered by the Stasi—the former East German secret service, who were jealous of his involvement with the KGB.

Burning to death is a very unusual method of committing suicide to use. Karl Koch was a man who had connections with the world of drugs. If he had decided to end it all, wouldn't he have chosen a more painless method?

GOVERNMENT AGENCIES

By breaking into top secret files, the hackers were threatening the national security of several countries. What role did the Soviet and U.S. governments play in the Internet Incident and what were their motives?

THE KGB

What data did the KGB want from the hackers? It appears they wanted information about defense technology. One of the primary functions of the KGB was to gather information about other countries. They were especially interested in countries whose governments were not considered friendly to the communist government of the Soviet Union—countries they thought they might one day have to fight. In other words, the West. They wanted to find out about any new defense systems that were being developed.

Therefore, the sites they pinpointed for the hackers to attack were mainly government offices, research laboratories, and companies specializing in micro-electronics projects. They included the Pentagon, NASA's Jet Propulsion Laboratory, and Lawrence Livermore research laboratories. The KGB particularly wanted to find out everything they could about a secret project concerning something called the "Megachip."

THE FBI

There is no doubt that the FBI played a very large part in tracking down the hackers. However, we don't know exactly *what* that part was. The case is recent enough for the files still to be classified today. What we do know is that Clifford Stoll, the systems administration manager at Berkeley Laboratories, alerted the FBI to the fact that he had found a hacker on the company's computers, and that the FBI wanted Stoll to give them as much information as he could find out. We also know that the FBI would not answer any of Stoll's questions. Up until this time, the FBI had not been aware of the dangers that hacking presented; it is thought that it was the Internet Incident that first alerted them to the enormous threat to national security of Internet crime.

COMPUTER HACKING

Computer hacking was already commonplace in the mid-1980s, when the Internet Incident took place. Up until then, the authorities had not really seen hacking as much of a threat. The general image of a computer hacker was that of a pimply teenager whiling away his time behind a computer screen. Except for the occasional appearance of a computer virus posted by a hacker on one of the world's numerous bulletin boards, the work of hackers was viewed as more mischievous than dangerous. But hacking was already becoming more organized, and therefore more dangerous. There have been many hacking gangs. Here are some of the most famous.

THE CHAOS CLUB

Founded in France in 1984, this group soon became well organized and established branches all over Germany. The main aim of the Chaos Club was to cause mischief by showing the authorities that their minimal security could be breached fairly easily. In 1985, the group hacked into the Bundespost, the German telephone service, and managed to install a program that enabled a bill of some 135,000 deutsche marks to be run up by continually dialing telephone numbers. Chaos' founder, Wau Holland, and another member of the group, Steffen Wernery, went to the press with their prank. The bill was never paid, but the ensuing publicity ensured that the Bundespost upped its security.

THE LEGION OF DOOM

The Legion of Doom is the United States' best-known gang of hackers. It was first heard of in 1984, when a hacker with the handle (pseudonym) of Superman's archenemy "Lex Luthor," set up a specialist hacker bulletin board in Florida named "Black Ice."

The original gang had only nine members, each with such handles as King Blotto, Agrajag the Prolonged, and Karl Marx. Over the years, the Legion of Doom has undergone several changes of personnel. Although it has never allowed membership to exceed 12 members, it is thought that about 40 different hackers have at some time or other belonged to the group.

The Legion of Doom is generally considered to be among the elite of the computer underground. In common with the Chaos Club in Germany, its aim is to create havoc on the digital network. And, like tough New York City street gangs who are known to use knives and guns as a means of protecting their territory, the Legion of Doom enforces a strict code of conduct among its members. For example, three gang members who conducted credit card fraud without the rest of the group's knowledge were made to suffer public humiliation over the global computer network.

Generally, The Legion of Doom is a fairly harmless presence on the Internet. Like its German counterparts, the group is more interested in exposing flaws in computer systems than in crime. Nevertheless, probably as a result of its chosen name, it is viewed with suspicion and distrust by the authorities.

DPAC

There are a number of rivals to the Legion of Doom, including a group known as "MoD"

(Masters of Destruction). But by far the most
serious rival is "DPAC," named after a Canadian
data communication system. DPAC came into
existence in the late 1980s and immediately found
itself in a computer war with the Legion of Doom.
The Legion of Doom disapproved of the new kids
on the block and began posting letters in
newsgroups that cast doubt on its rival's hacking
abilities. DPAC retaliated with the declaration of
war on the superhighway. However, dramatic as it
sounded, it turned out to be a bloodless war with
no real casualties. The conflict limited itself to
threatening letters left on bulletin boards, Legion
of Doom members' personal computers being
tampered with, and the lowering of one hacker's
personal credit rating.

THE BANK SCAM
Allegedly the most successful robbery ever
undertaken by computer hackers occurred in
1990. The crime was committed on a leading New
York City bank in order to impress the Legion of
Doom. Only two hackers were involved.
The beginnings of the plan came when one of the
hackers noticed that several major financial
institutions used "x.25" networks to transfer their
money. Using a process known as EFT (Electronic
Fund Transfer), the x.25 networks are operated
by commercial carriers and considered
impregnable. But the hackers believed they had
found a flaw in the system. They figured that
money being transferred using this protocol could
be intercepted before completion of the transaction
and diverted elsewhere. After setting up false
bank accounts, the money could then be
withdrawn before anyone had noticed that it was
missing.
    Putting their plan into action, the pair began

systematically hacking into bank computers until they could locate a machine that was running an EFT operation. They were sure that such a machine would be used by banks to transfer large amounts of capital. After several days of searching they found what they were looking for. Their next step was to monitor the EFT machine they had found in an effort to comprehend its transfer protocols. In other words, they needed to understand the language that the computer was using before they themselves could communicate with it. It did not take them long to crack this code.

Everything was going according to plan. The next step was for the hackers to contact a crooked accountant who had already opened a numbered Swiss bank account for them in a false name. The accountant had been skeptical of the scheme when the hackers had first told him about it. However, when they told him they were ready to wire the $50,000 minimum needed to keep up the account, he began to take their proposal more seriously. Several days later the accountant completed the transaction for the hackers— incidentally, upping his usual fee from $1,500 to $6,500!

The two hackers then traveled to Oklahoma. There they visited the hall of records and obtained new birth certificates. With these they acquired new Oklahoma IDs and Social Security numbers, which enabled them to open six different bank accounts in Houston and Dallas. They were now ready to begin their attack.

Early next day they hacked into their chosen target's computer and managed to divert a large financial transaction to an unused network computer terminal they had noticed. Taking turns at the computer, the two repeated this action until noon, making sure that the bank's financial transactions appeared to be operating as normal. When the attack was over, the pair had $184,000 under their control. Back at their computer terminal, the hackers now transferred the money to their Swiss bank account. They then gave instructions for the money to be transferred from that account to their six false accounts. In payments of $7,333, the amount was below the sum that required notification to the authorities. Over the next week, they withdrew $5,000 per day, until only $1,000 was left in each account. In total, the pair claim they managed to steal $66,000 in cash.

Nobody really knows if there is any truth in this tale. The New York City bank implicated in the case refuses to confirm or deny the story. What is undeniable, however, is that only days after the supposed scam, the hackers had already posted details of their escapade on Black Ice, The Legion of Doom's secret bulletin board. It was assumed that if the pair of hackers did not belong already to the Legion of Doom, they were attempting to impress the elite of the elite.

THE DARK AVENGER

In early October 1990, staff at the library of Britain's House of Commons noticed something strange happening to their computers. For no particular reason files would be lost, or parts of files they had been working on would disappear. When the problems refused to go away, an outside specialist was called in to take a look at the library's network of machines. It did not take the specialist long to realize that the library had been hit by a computer virus. After a detailed examination of the computers, he was able to find the piece of program code containing the virus. Upon inspection he discovered that the word "Nomenklatura" was contained within it.

With some research it was discovered that the word was of Russian origin. Nomenklatura was a term used to describe top members of the Soviet Communist Party who enjoyed special privileges such as cars and luxury accommodation. But the virus did not originate from the Soviet Union. Upon closer scrutiny, the program code was found to contain a string of text characters that appeared to be a message in another foreign language.

British researcher Alan Solomon, who was a programming specialist and ran a data retrieval service, was brought in to take a look at the code. He had a hunch that the language was Bulgarian. To confirm his suspicions he called up a bulletin board in Bulgaria and made contact with someone he thought might be able to translate the code. Bulletin boards exist throughout the world as smaller cousins to the Internet. Usually run by home enthusiasts from a modest personal computer, they serve the purpose of linking together computer devotees. They usually contain collections of software and digital conferences. Although it is perfectly possible to access bulletin boards all over the globe by simply dialing their telephone numbers and connecting via a modem, in practice this is too expensive. Unlike the Internet, which enables the user to access the world for the price of a local phone call, users of bulletin boards have no choice but to pay the full international telephone charge. For this reason, bulletin board members are usually local users.

A translation of the computer code in question confirmed that Solomon's intuition had been correct—the text was indeed written in Bulgarian.

There was a simple reason why Solomon had guessed that the virus had originated in Bulgaria. Over a period of many years Bulgaria had established a reputation as being the virus capital of the world. Many researchers even suspected that there might be a secret "virus factory" somewhere in Bulgaria. Solomon also had good reason to believe that he knew the name of the author of Nomenklatura. He had a hunch that the virus was written by the "Dark Avenger."

In the early 1980s, the Bulgarian president, Todor Zhivok, decided that his country was to become a center for high-tech development. Bulgaria, he announced, would be a major exporter of computers and electronic devices. However, the underdeveloped Bulgarian economy could not possibly hope to match its bold leader's words. In an attempt to speed up this technological development, the country began mass-producing poorly manufactured copies, or "clones," of IBM and Apple computers. These machines used pirated copies of operating systems and were inferior both in quality and speed. But while Bulgaria's hardware was obviously substandard, the brains behind their software were rapidly catching up with the West.

In 1989, the first Bulgarian viruses began to appear in Europe. The "Yankee Doodle" virus, which irritated computer users by playing them a tinny version of the title song from the Jimmy Cagney movie of the same name, proved to be fairly harmless. So did the "Jerusalem" virus, whose promise of wiping the host computer's hard drive on each Friday the 13th of the year turned out to be no more than an empty threat. The "Den Zuk" virus, a mixture of the author's first name Denny, and Zuko, the surname of character played by John Travolta in the movie *Grease*, was also fairly harmless. Except for changing the name of the computer's hard drive to "Y.C.i.E.R.P." it, too, did nothing to harm the user's computer.

However, the innocent nature of these Bulgarian viruses was to change on January 15, 1991, with the discovery of the "Casino" virus. On that date, computers belonging to the leading bank in the Mediterranean island of Malta were hit by a particularly virulent virus. The first evidence of the virus came from a message that was flashed on the computer screen that read:

DISK DESTROYER—A SOUVENIR OF MALTA
I have just DESTROYED the FAT on your disk!!
However, I have kept a copy in RAM, and I'm
giving you a last chance to restore your precious
data.
WARNING: IF YOU RESET NOW ALL YOUR DATA
WILL BE LOST FOREVER!!
Your data depends on a game of JACKPOT
CASINO DE MALTE JACKPOT
+L+ +?+ +C+
CREDITS: 5
"ANY KEY TO PLAY"

What the virus was inviting its unlucky hosts to do was, in fact, gamble the contents of their hard drive. Computer users had no choice but to take part in a game similar to the one featured on slot machines in amusement arcades. They had, basically, a one-in-three chance of success. They were given five chances to try to get three L's. If they managed to do this, the data on their computer would be saved and show the message:
You're lucky this time—but for your own sake, now
SWITCH OFF YOUR COMPUTER AND DON'T TURN
IT ON UNTIL TOMORROW!!!

Three ?s would result in the virus destroying all the data on the hard drive, while those unlucky enough to draw three Cs would not only lose their computer data but also receive an obscene message.

In June 1991 a major financial services company in the northeastern United States began to have problems with its computers. It was a secretary who first noticed that none of the documents she had been working on would print out. When the company's computer support team was called in to investigate, they wasted hours poring over the files. Eventually they declared that the company had been hit by a computer virus. The virus appeared to attack nothing but word processing documents; after a call to the producer of the word processing program, it was suggested that the technical team examine each of the infected files in great detail. Such an examination entails a painstaking search of all the files' computer codes and can take months to do thoroughly.

However, the technical team got lucky. Within the codes, the staff discovered the words:

This program was written in the city of Sofia 1988-1989 © Dark Avenger.

It was the first recorded instance of a name that would forever baffle serious computer users around the world.

A virus writer's conceit is usually in proportion to the damage that their malignant virus is capable of. Many writers leave a signature somewhere in their code as a gesture of defiance and warped pride in their work. But very few leave a message showing the time and place of the virus's birth.

And there were further surprises in store for the team investigating the Dark Avenger's virus. Scarcely visible within the gaggle of letters and symbols inside the code were the words "Diana P."

Nobody could understand the significance of this name. Perhaps, it was decided, the name belonged to the girlfriend of the author of the virus. However, one of the investigators had come across the virus before. Then, it was called simply, "Eddie."

Before a conclusion could be made on this latest puzzle, there was work to be done. The Dark Avenger's virus turned out to be extremely virulent. All attempts at producing an antidote to this dangerous piece of code proved to be useless, and it was finally decided that all 60 infected machines on the company's network would be turned off. Every one of the company's 2,200 computers would have to be checked—it was an undertaking that saw a team of 12 people working 12 hours a day. After 6,700 hours of intensive effort, the technical support team felt confident that they had eliminated all traces of the virus. However, within a week it was back and the whole process had to be repeated again. If this was not enough, the virus paid the company a third visit before finally disappearing for good.

When the damage to the company in time, manpower, and lost business was added up, it was found that the Dark Avenger had cost the company $1 billion.

Since 1988 about 200 viruses have been produced by Bulgaria. These include the "Version" series of viruses, the "Ping-Pong boot-sector" virus, the "Cascade" virus, and the "Nina" virus. However, by far the most celebrated writer of viruses remains the Dark Avenger. Like some latter-day Lone Ranger, the Dark Avenger refuses to remove his mask. He remains anonymous, a murky figure lurking on the edge of the digital highway. A name forever associated with disorder, dismay, and despair.

It is thought that the Dark Avenger produced his

first virus in September 1988. He has even written about his early hacking:

In those days there were no viruses in Bulgaria, so I decided to write the first. In early March 1989 it came into existence and started to live its own life and to terrorize all engineers and other suckers.

Among hackers and virus writers, the Dark Avenger has become something of a legend. This was evident in November 1990 when the world's first "virus exchange" was started in Sofia. Eventually copied all over the world, the bulletin board, or BBS, described itself as:

A place for free exchange of viruses and a place where everything is permitted!

A month after its inception, on November 28, 1990, the Dark Avenger logged into the virus exchange for the first time.

I'm glad to see this BBS is running, I've uploaded a couple of viruses to you. I hope you will give me access to the virus area.

When it was learned that the Dark Avenger was frequenting the BBS, other users began to bombard him with messages and give him VIP treatment. From this it was learned that the text string "Diana P" found in the "Eddie" virus and previously thought to be a reference to a girlfriend, actually referred to Diana, Princess of Wales. It was assumed that the Dark Avenger had something of a crush on Britain's troubled royal!

It was also discovered that the Dark Avenger was a fan of heavy metal music. The name Eddie apparently referred to the skeletal mascot used in British hard rock band Iron Maiden's stage acts. In common with the group, the Dark Avenger is obsessed with Satanism and peppers his viruses with similar references. His "Number of the Beast" virus contains the signature "666" from the *Book of Revelations*. Other Iron Maiden song titles have also been adopted as virus names. These include "Somewhere in Time," "The Evil that Men Do," and "The Good Die Young." In all, the Dark Avenger had written four different versions of the Eddie virus. He has also written six versions of "Number of the Beast." Other viruses include "Anthrax"—the name of another heavy metal group—and "Nomenklatura"—the virus that attacked the British House of Commons. Having attained superstar status in the virus world, the Dark Avenger has shown that he can't take criticism. In early 1991 he sent this message to Fidonet, the international bulletin board network:

Hello, all antivirus "researchers" who are reading this message—I am glad to inform you that my friends and I are developing a new virus that will mutate in one of 4,000,000,000 different ways! It will not contain any constant information. No virus scanner could detect it—[it's] undetectable and very destructive!

His words brought a hail of negative comments from understandably concerned computer users. The Dark Avenger's reaction was both swift and childishly vulgar. His critics were rewarded with a written reply full of profanities.

The identity of the Dark Avenger has never been established. And despite the protests of computer users around the world, this situation is unlikely to change. The Dark Avenger continues to bombard the information superhighway with his virulent viruses. There is nothing to stop him. Virus writing is not illegal in Bulgaria.

Epilogue

The last few decades have seen enormous advances in new technology. More and more organizations all over the world rely on computers to store and retrieve their information. And the more we rely on computers, the more dangerous the possibilities of computer crime become.

It was probably only a matter of time before someone hit upon the idea of using computers for spying.

There are still many mysteries hanging over the story of the Internet Incident. We don't know exactly what part the FBI played in the downfall of the gang of computer spies. Perhaps we'll never know what would have happened if they had not been stopped when they were. And perhaps we'll never know the truth about how Karl Koch died.

It is certainly true that since the Internet Incident, security measures worldwide have been tightened up dramatically. But computer users are becoming smarter all the time.

Maybe it could happen again.

CLASSIFIED

Reader, your mission is to be on the alert for the following spine-tingling books.

CLASSIFIED SERIES:

Prepare for further titles. Over and out.